COUNTRY TIME

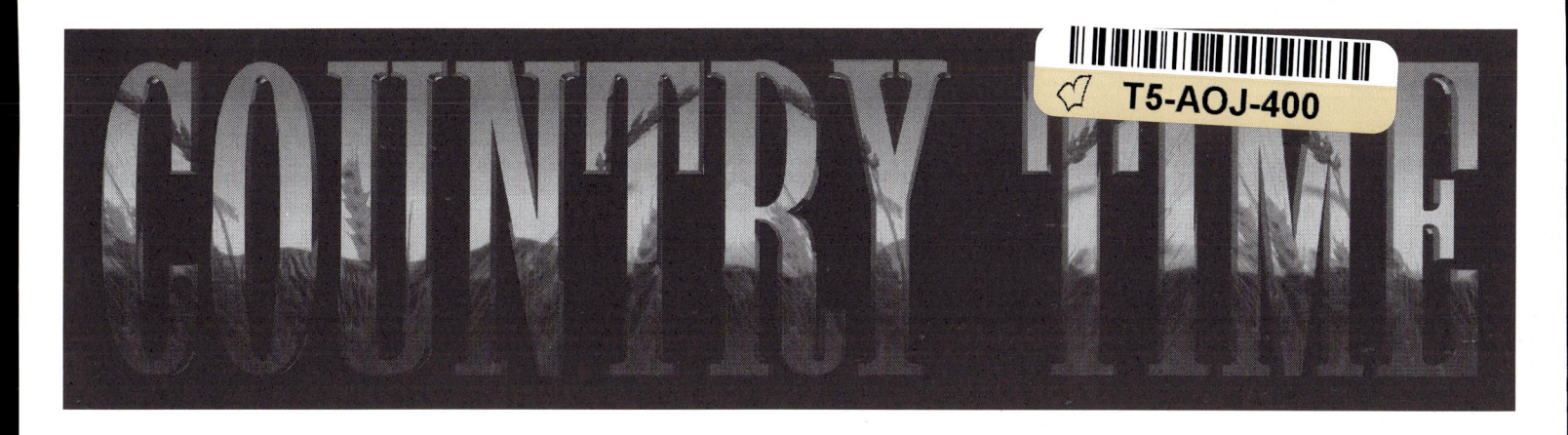

This publication is not for sale in
the EC and/or Australia
or New Zealand.

ISBN 0-7935-1969-1

HAL•LEONARD
CORPORATION
7777 W. BLUEMOUND RD. P.O. BOX 13819 MILWAUKEE, WI 53213

Copyright © 1992 by HAL LEONARD PUBLISHING CORPORATION
International Copyright Secured   All Rights Reserved

For all works contained herein:
Unauthorized copying, arranging, adapting, recording or public performance is an infringement of copyright.
Infringers are liable under the law.

COUNTRY TIME

CONTENTS

4	Achy Breaky Heart	Billy Ray Cyrus
10	After All This Time	Rodney Crowell
14	Anymore	Travis Tritt
26	Battle Hymn Of Love, The	Kathy Mattea & Tim O'Brien
19	Black Velvet	Robin Lee
34	Boot Scootin' Boogie	Brooks & Dunn
38	Brand New Man	Brooks & Dunn
43	Brotherly Love	Keith Whitley & Earl Thomas Conley
50	Can't Stop My Heart From Lovin' You	O'Kanes
62	Can't Stop Myself From Loving You	Patty Loveless
55	Chasin' That Neon Rainbow	Alan Jackson
66	Chill Of An Early Fall, The	George Strait
72	Crying My Heart Out Over You	Ricky Scaggs
76	Deeper Than The Holler	Randy Travis
82	Down At The Twist And Shout	Mary-Chapin Carpenter
89	Faded Love	Willie Nelson & Ray Price
92	Fool Such As I, A	Hank Snow/Baillie & The Boys
96	Forty Hour Week (For A Livin')	Alabama
101	Golden Ring	George Jones
104	He Talks To Me	Lorrie Morgan
108	Here's A Quarter (Call Someone Who Cares)	Travis Tritt
114	Houston Solution	Ronnie Milsap
120	I Feel Lucky	Mary-Chapin Carpenter
126	I Meant Every Word He Said	Ricky Van Shelton
130	I Thought It Was You	Doug Stone
135	I Won't Take Less Than Your Love	Tanya Tucker
142	If The Devil Danced (In Empty Pockets)	Joe Diffie

147	In A Different Light	Doug Stone
152	Is It Raining At Your House	Vern Gosdin
156	It Ain't Nothin'	Keith Whitley
160	Keep It Between The Lines	Ricky Van Shelton
166	Life's Too Long (To Live Like This)	Ricky Skaggs
173	Love Will Find Its Way To You	Reba McEntire
180	Mama Tried	Merle Haggard
182	Mirror Mirror	Diamond Rio
192	My Arms Stay Open All Night	Tanya Tucker
187	My Next Broken Heart	Brooks & Dunn
196	One Promise Too Late	Reba McEntire
202	Only Here For A Little While	Billy Dean
214	Restless	Mark O'Connor & The New Nashville Cats
209	Rumor Has It	Reba McEntire
220	Shameless	Garth Brooks
226	She And I	Alabama
230	Someday	Alan Jackson
236	Somewhere In My Broken Heart	Billy Dean
240	Strong Enough To Bend	Tanya Tucker
245	Sunday Kind Of Love, A	Reba McEntire
250	Tempted	Marty Stuart
255	(Smooth As) Tennessee Whiskey	George Jones
260	Thanks Again	Ricky Skaggs
265	There For A While	Steve Wariner
270	There's A Tear In My Beer	Hank Williams Sr. & Jr.
272	These Lips Don't Know How To Say Goodbye	Doug Stone
276	Things Are Tough All Over	Shelby Lynn
286	This One's Gonna Hurt You (For A Long, Long Time)	Marty Stuart & Travis Tritt
292	'Til A Tear Becomes A Rose	Keith Whitley & Lorrie Morgan
281	Turn It Loose	The Judds
298	Turn It On, Turn It Up, Turn Me Loose	Dwight Yoakam
303	When You Say Nothing At All	Keith Whitley
308	Whiskey Ain't Workin', The	Marty Stuart & Travis Tritt
314	Whole Lotta Holes	Kathy Mattea
318	Woman Before Me, The	Trisha Yearwood
322	You Again	The Forester Sisters
332	You Don't Count The Cost	Billy Dean
327	You Know Me Better Than That	George Strait

ACHY BREAKY HEART
(a.k.a. DON'T TELL MY HEART)

Words and Music by
DON VON TRESS

what a fool I've been and laugh and joke a-bout me on the
fist can tell my lip. He nev-er real-ly liked me an-y-

A

phone. You can tell my arms go
way. Or tell your Aunt Lou-ise. Tell

back to the farm. You can tell my feet to hit the
an-y-thing you please. My-self al-read-y knows I'm not o-

E

floor. Or you can tell my lips to
kay. Or you can tell my eyes to

tell my fin-ger-tips they won't be reach-ing out for you no more.
watch out for my mind. It might be walk-ing out on me to-day.

But Don't tell my heart, my ach-y break-y heart. I just don't think he'd un-der-stand. And if you tell my heart, my ach-y break-y heart, he might blow_ up and kill this man. Ooh._____

man.

Don't tell my heart, my ach-y break-y heart. I just don't think he'd under-stand. And if you tell my heart, my ach-y break-y heart, he might blow up and kill this man. Ooh.

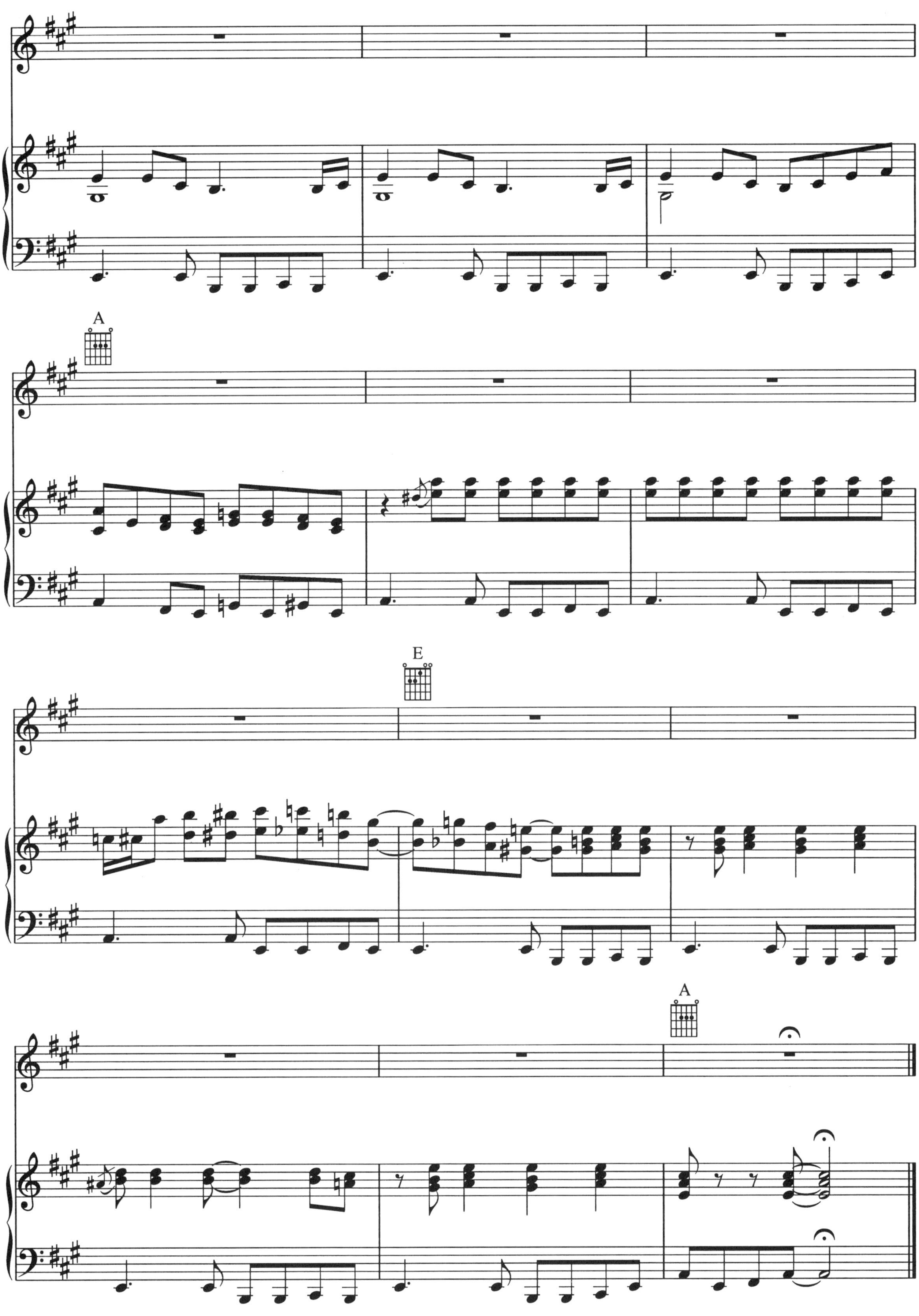
A
E
A

AFTER ALL THIS TIME

Words and Music by
RODNEY CROWELL

Slowly

There were trains and we out-run 'em. There were
rain that we out-last-ed. There was

songs and we out-sung 'em. There were
pain, but we got past it. There were

bright - er days nev - er
last good - byes still left un -

end - ing. There was
spo - ken. There were

time and we were burn-ing. There were
ways I should have thrilled you. There were

rhymes and we were learn - ing. There was
days when I could have killed you. You're the

all the love two hearts could hold.
on - ly love my life has known.

And af-ter all __ this time, you're
And af-ter all __ this time, you're
D.S. Instrumental

al - ways on my mind. __
al - ways on my mind. __ Hey,
And

I could nev - er let it end, 'cause my heart takes so long to mend. The
I could nev - er let you go, a bro - ken heart that heals so slow, could
I could nev - er let it in, cause my heart takes so long to mend. The

dream that keeps your hopes _ a - live, the lone - ly nights _ you hold in - side. _ And
nev - er beat for some - one new while you're a - live _ and I am too. _ And
dream that keeps your hopes _ a - live, the lone - ly nights _ you hold in - side. _ And

13

ANYMORE

Words and Music by TRAVIS TRITT
and JILL COLUCCI

Moderately slow

I can't hide the way I feel about
one last ap-peal to show

you an-y-more.
you how I feel a-bout you. Mm hm.

I could hold the hurt in-side, keep the pain
'Cause there's no - one else I swear holds a can-

Copyright © 1991 Tree Publishing Co., Inc., Post Oak Publishing, EMI April Music Inc. and Heartland Express Music
All Rights on behalf of Tree Publishing Co., Inc. and Post Oak Publishing
Administered by Sony Music Publishing, 8 Music Square West, Nashville, TN 37203
International Copyright Secured   All Rights Reserved

_out of my eyes__ an - y - more.__
-dle an - y - where_ next to you.__ Mm hm._

My tears no lon - ger wait-
My heart can't take the beat-

-ing._ My re - sis - tance ain't_ that strong._
-ing__ not hav - ing you_ to hold._

My mind keeps re - cre - at - ing__ a love with you_ a - lone._
A small voice keeps re - peat - ing__ deep in - side_ my soul._

And I'm tired of pretending
It says I can't keep pretending
I don't love you anymore.
I don't love you anymore. Let me make
I've got to take the chance or let it pass by
if I expect to get on with my life.

My tears no longer wait-ing. Oh, my re-sis-tance ain't that strong.

G
F
Oh, my mind keeps re - cre - at -
G
E/G♯
Am
F
G
- ing a love with you a - lone.
And I'm tired of pre - tend - ing
F
G
C
F
I don't love you an - y - more.
An - y - more.
C
F
C
An - y - more.
rit.

BLACK VELVET

Moderately slow bluesy shuffle (♩♩ played as ♩♪ triplet)

Vocal 2nd time only

Words and Music by CHRISTOPHER WARD
and DAVID TYSON

Jim- mie Rod - gers on the Vic - trola up high.
"White Light - nin'" bound to drive you wild.

Ma- ma's danc - in' with ba - by on her shoul - der.
Ma- ma's ba - by is in the heart of ev - 'ry school girl.

The sun is set - tin' like mo - las - ses in the sky.
"Love Me Ten - der" leaves 'em cry - in' in the aisle.

B7sus   B7   A7sus   A7

The boy could sing; knew how to move ev - 'ry - thing.
The way he moved it was a sin so sweet and true.

G7sus
G7
Dsus
Al- ways want - ing more. __
He'd leave you long - ing for __
Am9
D
Black vel - vet and that lit - tle boy __ smile. __
Am9
F
C
Black vel - vet {with / and} that slow south-ern style.
Am9
D
A new re - li - gion __ that - 'll bring you __ to your knees.

1
C7
B7sus
Em
Black vel - vet, if you please.
2
C7
B7sus
Black vel - vet, if you
Em
please.
Am
Ev-'ry word of ev-'ry song
B7
Em7
that he sang was for you.

In a flash he was gone, it happened so soon. What could you do?

Am7
Am9
Black vel - vet and that
D
Am7
Am9
lit - tle boy smile.
Black vel - vet in that
F
C
Am7
Am9
slow south-ern style.
A new re - li - gion that - 'll
D
1
C7
B7sus
4
bring you to your knees.
Black vel - vet,

Em
C7
B7sus
if you please.
Black vel - vet, if you
Em7
please.
If you please.
If you please.
If you please.
Mm.
Mm.
Repeat ad lib. and Fade

THE BATTLE HYMN OF LOVE

Words and Music by DON SCHLITZ and PAUL OVERSTREET

Bright Country two beat

(Female:) I will

pledge my heart to the love we share,
sake my rest for your hap-pi-ness.

through the good and the bad times
Till my death, I will stand by

© Copyright 1987 by MCA MUSIC PUBLISHING, A Division of MCA INC., DON SCHLITZ MUSIC, SCREEN GEMS-EMI MUSIC and SCARLET MOON MUSIC
Rights of DON SCHLITZ MUSIC administered by MCA MUSIC PUBLISHING, A Division of MCA INC., 1755 Broadway, New York, NY 10019
International Copyright Secured   All Rights Reserved

MCA music publishing

too.
you.   I for-   (Both:) With

God as my wit-ness, this vow I will make: "To have and to hold you, no oth-er to take."

E
A
(Female:) For rich or for poor, un - der skies
D
gray or blue, (Both:) till my
A
E
A
death I will stand by you.
(Male:) There are

wars and there are ru - mors. Wars yet to come. Tempt - ta - tions we'll have to walk through. Though oth - ers may trem - ble, I

will not run. Till my death, I will stand by you. *(Both:)* I will put on the ar - mor of faith - ful - ness to fight for a heart that is true. *(Male:)* Till the bat- tle is ___ won ___ I will not rest. ___ *(Both:)* Till my death I will stand by ___ you. With

D.S. al Coda

CODA
E
A
rich or for poor, under
D
A
skies gray or blue till my death I will
E
A
stand by you. Till the bat -
A
- tle is won I will not

run.____ Till my death I ____ will stand by ____

you.

BOOT SCOOTIN' BOOGIE

Words and Music by
RONNIE DUNN

Moderate Shuffle

Out in the coun-try past the
Got a good job, I work hard
Instrumental solo
bar-ten-der asks me, says,

cit-y lim-it sign, well there's a hon-ky tonk near the
for my mon-ey. When it's quit-tin' time, I
"Son, what will it be?" I want a shot at that red-head yon-der

coun-ty line. The joint starts jump-in' ev-'ry
hit the door run-nin'. I fire up my pick-up truck
look-in' at me. The dance floor's hop-pin' and it's

Copyright © 1991 Tree Publishing Co., Inc. and Alfred Avenue Music
All Rights on behalf of Tree Publishing Co., Inc. Administered by Sony Music Publishing, 8 Music Square West, Nashville, TN 37203
International Copyright Secured   All Rights Reserved

night when the sun goes down. They got whis-
and let the horses run. I go fly-
hot-ter than the Fourth of Ju-ly. I see out-

-key, women, music and smoke. It's
in' down that high-way to that hide-a-way
-laws, in-laws, crooks and straights

where all the cow-boy folk go to boot scoot-in'
stuck out in the woods, to do the boot scoot-in'
all out mak-in' it shake do-in' the boot scoot-in'

boo-gie. I've
boo-gie. *Solo ends* The Yeah,
boo-gie.

A
heel to toe, do - cie doe, come on ba - by, let's go
E
boot scoot-in'!
Woh, _
A
Cad - il - lac, Black - jack,
ba - by meet me out back, we're gon-na
E
boo-gie.
Oh, _
B7
get down turn a-round, _ go to town, _ boot scoot-in'

E
1
D.S.
2
boo-gie.
Woh,
3
B7
I said, get down, turn a-round, go to town, boot scoot-in'
E
B7
boo-gie.
Woh, get down, turn a-round,
no chord
E
A
E
go to town, boot scoot-in' boo-gie.

BRAND NEW MAN

Words and Music by DON COOK,
RONNIE DUNN and KIX BROOKS

Moderate Country Rock

I saw the light, I've been bap-tised by the fire in your touch and the flame in your eyes. I'm born to love a-gain, I'm a brand new man.

Copyright © 1991 Tree Publishing Co., Inc., Cross Keys Publishing Co., and Fort Kix Music
All Rights Administered by Sony Music Publishing, 8 Music Square West, Nashville, TN 37203
International Copyright Secured   All Rights Reserved

Well, the whole town's talkin' 'bout the line I'm walkin' that leads right to your door. Oh, how I used to roam, I was a rolling stone.

love 'em and leave 'em, oh. I'd brag about my freedom, how no one could tie me down. Then I met you, now my heart beats true. Baby,

used to have a wild side, they say a country mile wide. I'd
you and me together feels more like forever than

burn those beer joints down. That's all changed now,
anything I've ever known. We're right on track,

you turned my life around.
I ain't a-lookin' back. Oh,

I saw the light, I've been baptised by the fire in your touch and the flame *in your eyes. I'm born to love a - gain, I'm a brand new man.*

I used to

CODA

Yeah, I saw the light, I've been

42

bap-tised by the fire in your touch__ and the flame__ in your eyes.__ I'm born__ to love__ a-gain,__ I'm a brand__ new__ man.__

Yeah, I'm born__ to love__ a-gain,__ I'm a brand__ new__ man.__

BROTHERLY LOVE

Words and Music by JIMMY STEWART
and TIM NICHOLS

Easy Country two-beat

We share the same last name
You hat-ed girls 'til I
They share the same last name

___ and the same color eyes,
___ had my first date.
___ and the same color eyes,

Copyright © 1989 Milsap Music, Inc., Talbot Music and Peer-International Company
Rights for Milsap Music, Inc. administered by Careers-BMG Music Publishing, Inc. (BMI)
International Copyright Secured   All Rights Reserved

but we fought like ti - gers over that old red bike.
I brought her home from the mov - ies, you stayed up late.
but they fight like ti - gers o - ver one old red bike.

"I'm bat - tin' first and you can't
Three on a couch
And look - in' at them re - minds

___ use my glove." It would-n't take long ___ 'til push ___
watch-in' T. V.; ___ I was smil-in' at her ___ while you were
___ me of us. They're gon-na fight ___ and they're ___

___ came to shove, ___ but we looked out ___ for each oth-
laugh-in' at me. ___ But I would-n't trade ___ it for noth-
___ gon-na fuss, ___ but they've got some-thin' spe-

-er with }
-in': } broth-er-ly love. ___
-cial, it's }

There's a bond that brothers know and it gets stronger as they grow, a love that time and miles

47

can't come between. We disagree, but in the end there will never be two closer friends and brotherly love is some-

-thin' we ___ all ___ need.

Yeah, they've got somethin' spe - cial, it's broth - er - ly love.

CAN'T STOP MY HEART FROM LOVIN' YOU

Words and Music by JAMIE O'HARA and KIERAN KANE

Lately your love is a cold, cold rain comin' down on self I'm a gonna go. I pull out my

G
C/G
G
C/G
me, always the same.
bag, I pack up my clothes.
G
C/G
G
C/G
G
C/G
Ev - er - y day
I write a note
G
C/G
G
C/G
G
C/G
is a cloud - y sky.
that says we're through.
But I just can't
But I al - ways
G
D7
D7sus
find a way to say good -
end up tear - in' it in

G
bye.
two.
I can't stop my
C Csus C C9
heart from lov - in'
G7 Bm/F♯ C/E
you, though you treat me
D D7sus G7
bad - ly and make me blue.

53

why, oh, why can't I leave?

What kind of hold do you have on me?

I can't stop my you.

CHASIN' THAT NEON RAINBOW

Words and Music by ALAN JACKSON
and JIM McBRIDE

Bright Country tempo

Dad-dy won a ra-di-o,___ He tuned it to a coun-try show.___ I was rock-in' in the cra-dle to the cry-in' of a steel___ gui-tar.

At-las and a cof-fee cup,___ five pick-ers and an old___ Dodge___ truck. Head-in' down to Hous-ton for a show on Sat-ur-day night.

Copyright © 1990 SEVENTH SON MUSIC, MATTIE RUTH MUSICK and EMI APRIL MUSIC INC.
International Copyright Secured   All Rights Reserved

G
Ma-ma used to sing to me. She
Well, this o - ver head is kill - in' me.
C
D
taught me that sweet har - mo - ny. Now she wor-ries,'cause she nev-er thought I
Half the time I sing for free. But when the crowd's in - to it, Lord it
C
G
D
ev - er real - ly take it this far, a - sing-in' in the bars and
makes this thing I'm do - in' seem right. Stand-in' in the spot - light
G
C
Chas - in' that ne - on rain - bow, liv - in' that hon - ky - tonk

dream.___ 'Cause all I've ev - er want - ed ___ is to pick this__ gui - tar and sing.___ Just try'n' to be __ some - bod - y.___ Just wan - na be heard__ and__ seen. I'm chas - in' that ne - on rain - bow,___ liv - in' that hon - ky - tonk ___

dream.

An

dream. Dad-dy had a ra-di-o. He won it thir-ty years a-go. He said,

"Son, I just know we're gonna hear you singin' on it some-day."

Well, I ___ made it up to Mu-sic Row, ___ but Lord-y, don't the wheels_ turn_ slow. Still, I would-n't trade a min-ute; I would-n't have it an-y oth-er way. ___ Just show me to the stage, I'm ___ chas-in' that ne-on rain-bow, I'm liv-in' that hon-ky-tonk dream. 'Cause all I've ev-er want-ed is to pick this guitar and sing. Just try'n' to be some-body. Just wan-na be heard and seen. I'm

chas - in' that ne - on rain - bow, ____ liv - in' that hon - ky - tonk ___ dream. Oh, I'm ___ chas - in' that ne - on ___ rain - bow, _____ liv - in' that hon - ky - tonk ____ dream. ____

Can't Stop Myself From Loving You

Words and Music by KOSTAS
and DEAN FOLKVORD

Moderate Country beat

Rain-drops fall from the sky, tear-drops fall from my eyes. Can't stop my- self from lov-ing you.

Copyright © 1991 Songs Of PolyGram International, Inc.
International Copyright Secured   All Rights Reserved

Your heart-ache's found a home, I walk these streets a-lone. Can't stop myself from lov-ing you. I know I should-n't waste my time in dreams of yes-ter-

They say that time can heal a lone-ly heart that's broke in

day. But your mem'-ry's ____ all ___ that I have left ____
two. But time ran ____ out on me the day ___ you

since you've ____ gone ___ a-way. No mat-ter
walked out ____ of ___ my world. So let ____ the

what ___ I do, ___ my heart ____ stays ___ cold ___ and blue.
tear-drops fall, ___ the rain ____ will ___ hide ___ them all.

Can't stop ____ my - self ____ from lov ____ ing ____
Can't stop ____ my - self ____ from lov ____ ing ____

you. _____ you, _____ can't stop ____ my-self ____ from lov - ing ____ you.

THE CHILL OF AN EARLY FALL

Words and Music by GREEN DANIEL
and GRETCHEN PETERS

Well, her old friend from her old end of town dropped by today.
No doubt it's gonna be cold out tonight, I've shivered all day. And when I

F C/E Dm F7/C
3
way down deep in - side me some - thing died when he came
look in her eyes, even to hold her so
3
G F/A G/B C7 B♭/D C/E
'round to see her that way. Here it
tight, she just looks a - way. Oh, she'll
F Am Dm F7
comes a - gain, that same old chil - ly wind will blow
swear that it's true, he's just some-one she knew long a -
B♭ F/A G Bdim7
like a cold win - ter squall,
go, but I'll know that's not all,
and I'll be -

gin to feel the chill of an ear-ly fall. And I'll be drink-in' a-gain and think-in' when-ev-er he calls. There's a storm comin' home

Dm F7/C G9 G7/B
and it won't be too long till the snow falls.
C7 B♭/D C/E F Am
Oh, I'll be so - ber some,
Dm F7/C B♭ F/A
but when Oc - to - ber comes and goes in no time
G Bdim7 F/C
at all, I'll be - gin to feel the

chill of an ear-ly fall. Oh, how quick they slip a-way, here to-day and gone to-mor-row. Lov-ing sea-sons nev-er stay, bit-ter winds are sure to fol-low.

Now there's fall.

Oh, I'll be-gin to feel the chill of an ear-ly fall.

poco rit.

CRYING MY HEART OUT OVER YOU

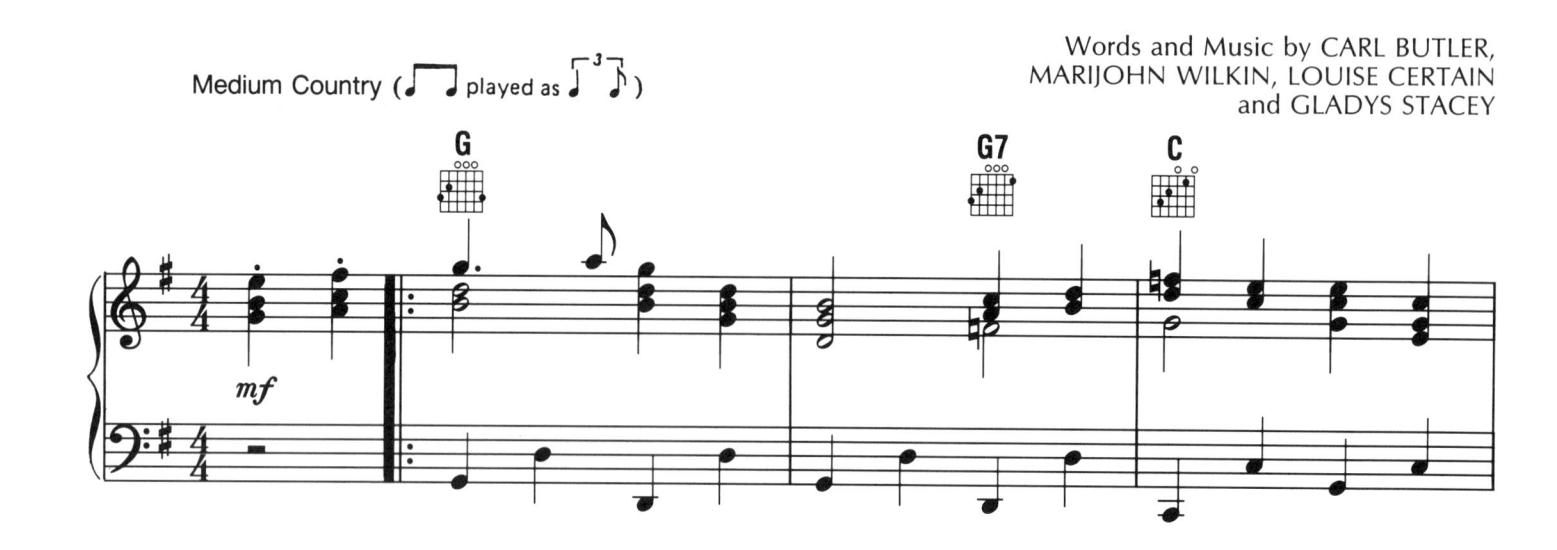

Words and Music by CARL BUTLER,
MARIJOHN WILKIN, LOUISE CERTAIN
and GLADYS STACEY

Medium Country (♪♪ played as ♪³♪)

Off some-where the mu-sic's play-ing soft and low,
Each night I climb the stairs up to my room,

Copyright © 1959 by Cedarwood Publishing
Copyright Renewed
International Copyright Secured   All Rights Reserved

D7
and an - oth - er holds the
it seems I hear you
G
one that I love so. I was blind,
whis - per in the gloom. I miss your pic -
G7 C
I could not see that you meant the world to me,
- ture on the wall, and your foot - steps in the hall
D7
but like a fool I stood and watched you go.
while I'm cry - ing my heart out o - ver you.
3

Lyrics:

Now I'm cry-ing my heart out o-ver you. Those blue eyes, now they smile at some-one new. Ev-er since you went a-way, I die a little more each day 'cause I'm cry-ing my heart out o-ver you.

you.

DEEPER THAN THE HOLLER

Words and Music by DON SCHLITZ and PAUL OVERSTREET

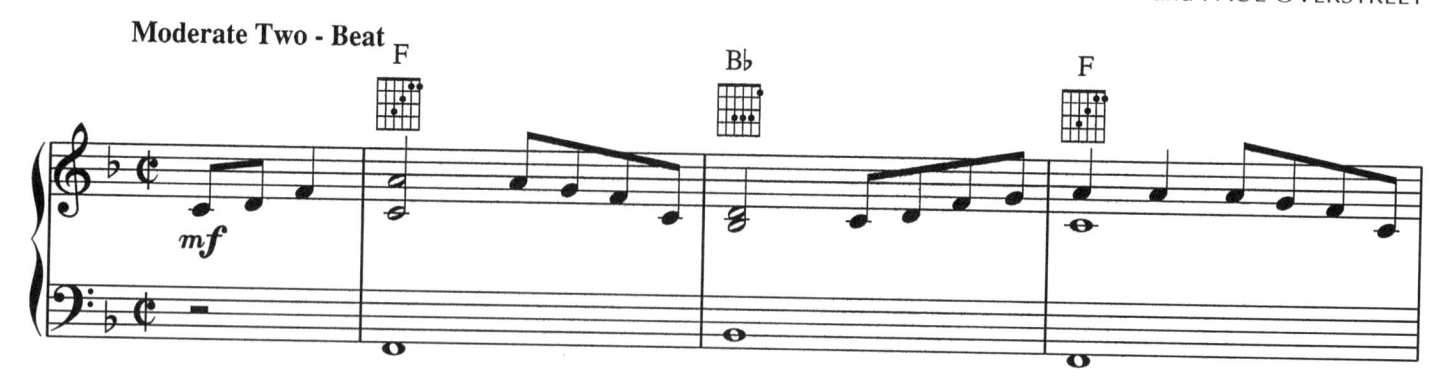

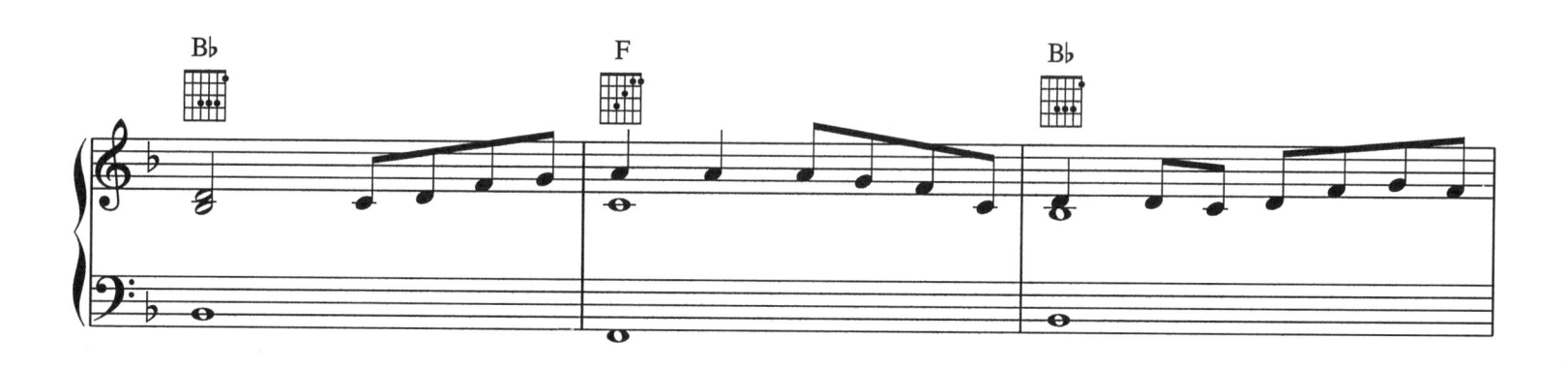

Moderate Two - Beat

Well, I heard those cit-y sing-

© Copyright 1988 by MCA MUSIC PUBLISHING, A Division of MCA INC., DON SCHLITZ MUSIC, SCREEN GEMS-EMI MUSIC, INC. and SCARLET MOON MUSIC.
Rights of DON SCHLITZ MUSIC administered by MCA MUSIC PUBLISHING, A Division of MCA INC., 1755 Broadway, New York, NY 10019.
International Copyright Secured   All Rights Reserved

-ers singing 'bout how they can love, Deeper than the oceans, higher than the stars above.

Well, I come from the country and I know I ain't seen it all, but I heard that ocean's back roads to the Broadway shows with a million miles between, there's at least a million

Bb F Bb F
salt - y and the stars they some - times fall. And
love songs that peo - ple love to sing. And
Gm
that would not do jus - tice to the way
ev - 'ry - one is diff - 'rent and ev -
Am Bb
I feel for you, so I had to sing a song
- ry - one's the same and this is just an - oth -
F/A Gm C
a - bout all the things I knew.
- er way of say - ing the same thing.

My love is deeper than the holler, stronger than the river, higher than the pine trees growing tall upon the hill. My love is purer than the snowflakes that fall in late Decem-

-ber, _____ And hon-est as __ a ro-bin __ on __ a spring-

-time win-dow sill, _____ And long-er than __ the song __

___ of a whip-poor-will. _____

From the _____

My love is a whip-poor-will.

DOWN AT THE TWIST AND SHOUT

Words and Music by
MARY-CHAPIN CARPENTER

Fast Country two-beat

Sat-ur-day night __ and the moon is out. __ I wan-na head on o-ver to the Twist and Shout, find a two-step part-ner and a ca-jun beat, when it lifts me up, __ I'm gon-na

© 1990 EMI APRIL MUSIC INC./GETAREALJOB MUSIC
All Rights Controlled and Administered by EMI APRIL MUSIC INC.
All Rights Reserved   International Copyright Secured   Used by Permission

find my feet out in the middle of a big dance floor. When I hear that fiddle, wanna beg for more. Wanna dance to a band from a-Louisian' tonight.

And I never have wandered down to New Orleans,
alligator stew and a crawfish pie, a
mama, bring your papa, bring your sister too. They got

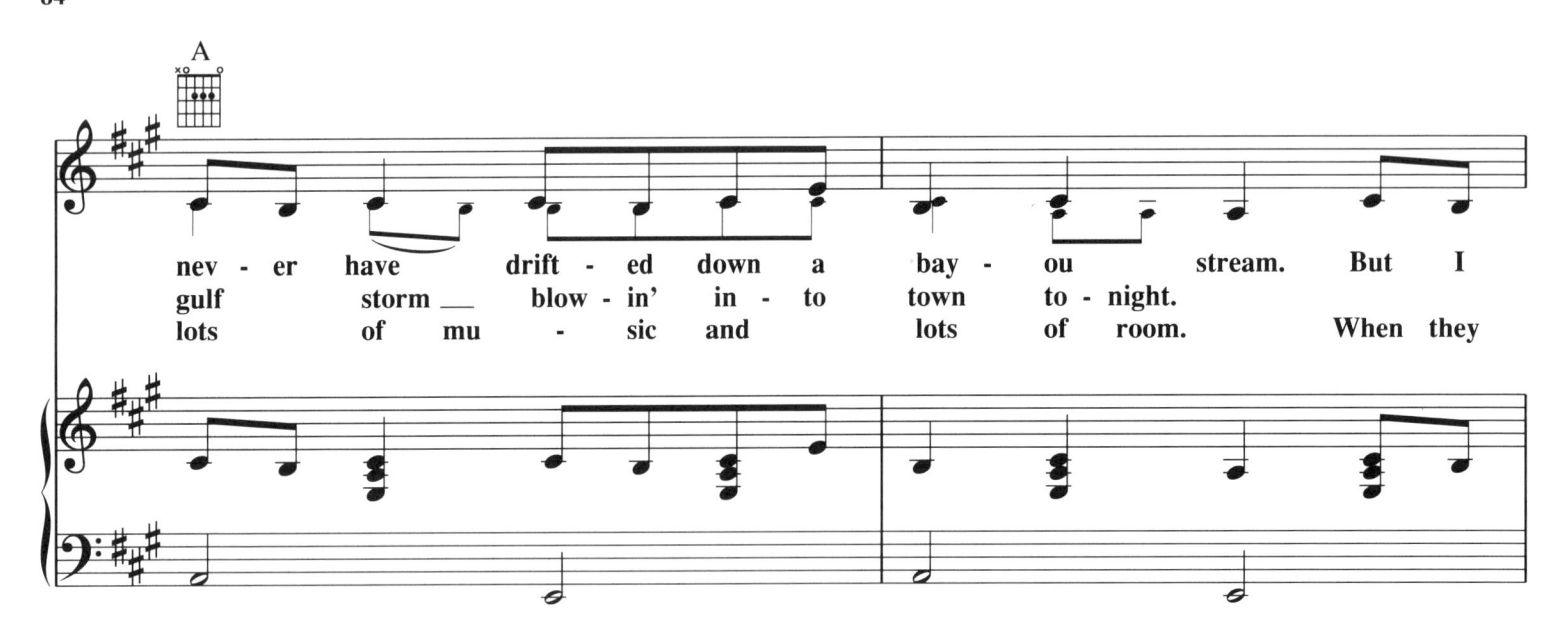

never have drift-ed down a bay-ou stream. But I
gulf storm blow-in' in-to town to-night.
lots of mu-sic and lots of room. When they

heard that mu-sic on the ra-di-o, and I
Liv-in' on the del-ta it's quite a show. They got hur-
play you a waltz from a nine-teen ten, you're

swore some-day I was gon-na go down a high-way 10, past a
-ri-cane par-ties ev-'ry time it blows. But here up north it's a
gon-na feel a lit-tle bit young a-gain. Well you learn to dance with your

Lafayette; there's a Bat - on Rouge. And I
cold, cold rain, and there ain't no cure for my
rock - in' roll, you learn to swing with

won't for - get to send you a card with my re - grets 'cause I'm
blues to - day; ex - cept when the pa - per says Beou - so - leil is a
do - si - do. But you learn to love at the fais do do when you

nev - er gon - na come back home.
com - in' in - to town. Ba - by, let's go down. It's
hear a lit - tle Jolie Blon.

Sat - ur - day night and the moon is out. I wan - na

head on o - ver to the Twist and Shout, find a two - step part - ner and a ca - jun beat. When it lifts me up, I'm gon - na find __ my feet out in the mid - dle of a big dance flloor. When I hear that fid - dle, wan - na beg for more. Wan - na dance to a band from a -

Loui - si - an'_____ to - night. Whoo! Hey!

Instrumental solo

Solo ends They got a *Solo ends* Bring your

To Coda ⊕

D.S. al Coda

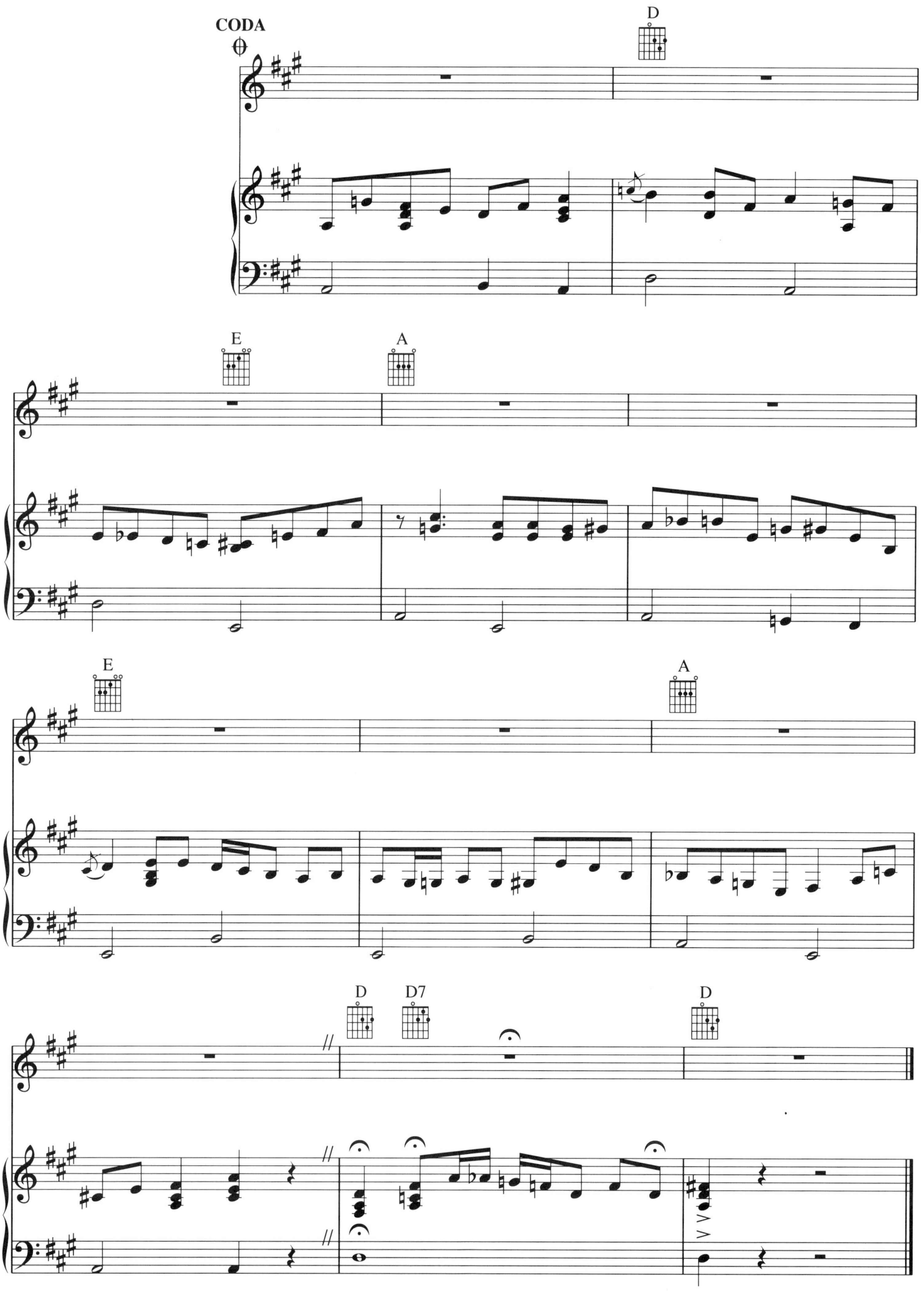
CODA
D
E
A
E
A
D
D7
D

FADED LOVE

Words and Music by JOHN WILLS
and BOB WILLS

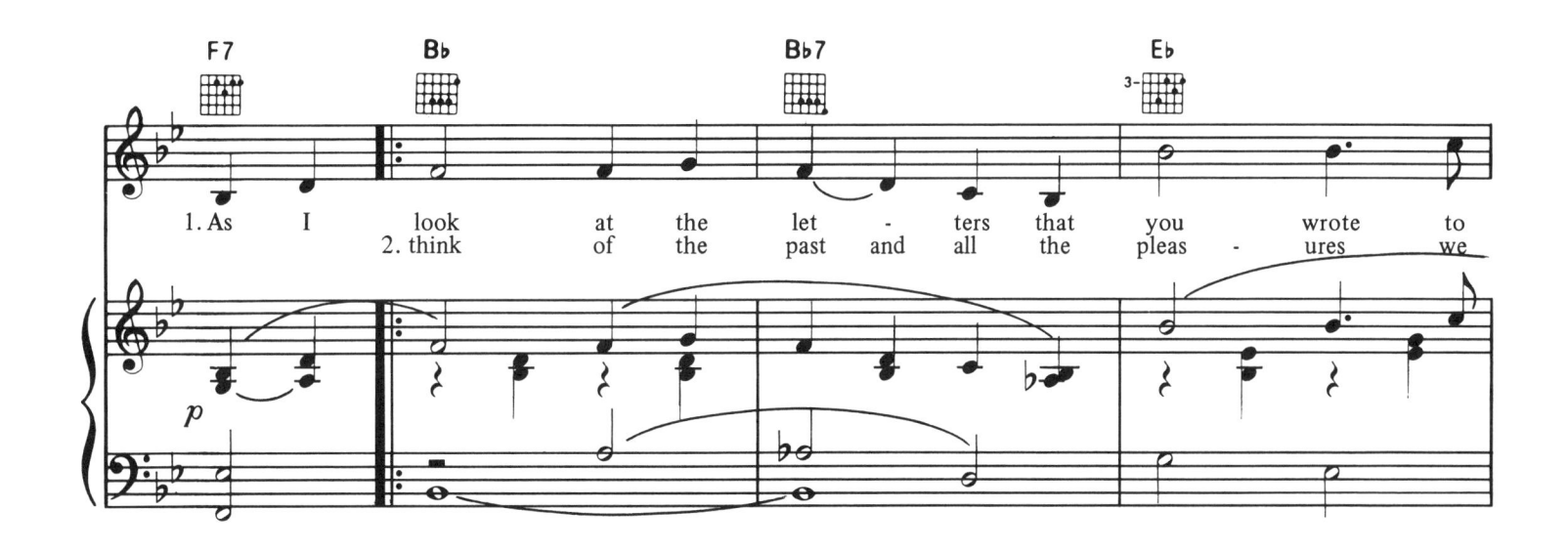

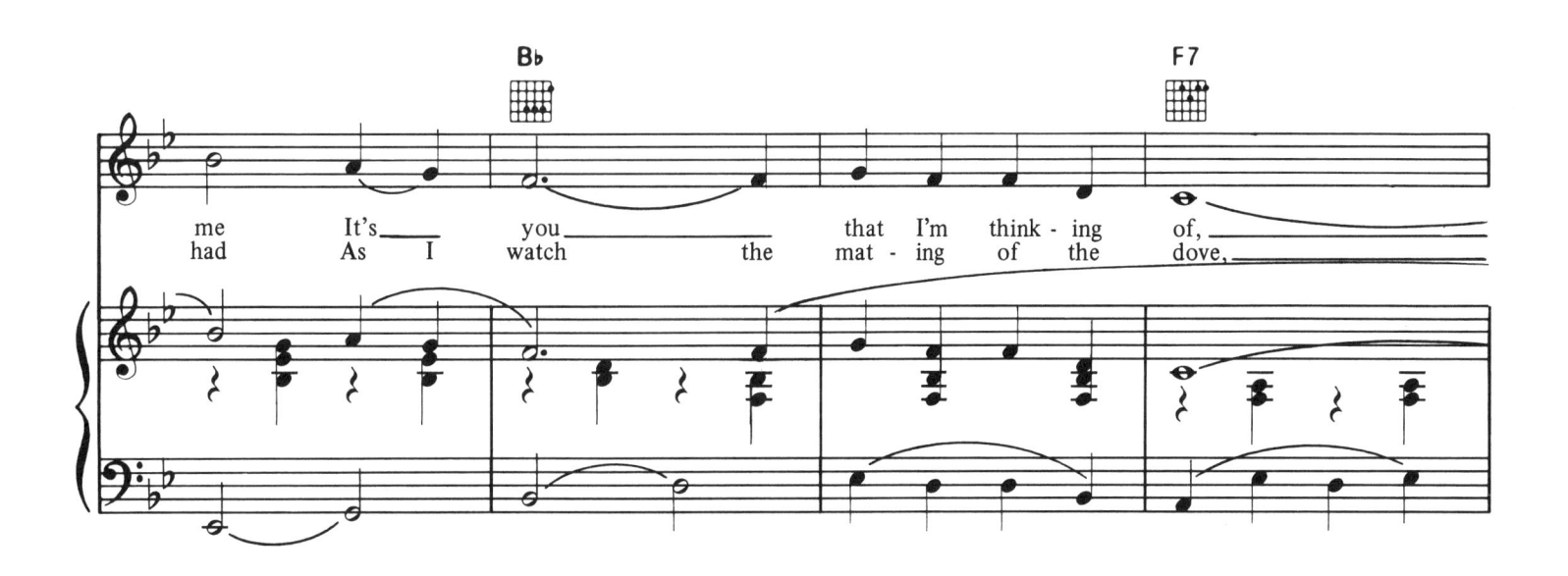

Moderato

1. As I look at the letters that you wrote to me, It's you that I'm thinking of,
2. think of the past and all the pleasures we had As I watch the mating of the dove,

Copyright © 1950, 1951 by Bob Wills Music, Inc.
Copyright Renewed, Assigned to Unichappell Music, Inc. (Rightsong Music, Publisher)
International Copyright Secured   All Rights Reserved

Bb
Bb7
As I read the lines that to
It was in the spring - time that
Eb
Bb
F7
me were so sweet I re - mem - ber our Fad - ed
you said good - bye, I re - mem - ber our Fad - ed
Bb
Chorus
Bb
Love.
Love.
I miss you
Eb
F7
dar - ling more and more ev - 'ry day As

Bb
F7
heav - en would miss the stars a - bove.
Bb
With ev - 'ry heart - beat I still
Eb
Bb
F7
think of you And re - mem - ber our Fad - ed
1 Bb
C#dim
F7
2 Bb7
Eb
Ebm
Bb
Love.
2. I
Love.
fz

(NOW AND THEN THERE'S) A FOOL SUCH AS I

Words and Music by
BILL TRADER

D7
Eb
Bb
love you dear until the day I die.
Now and then
F7
Bb
there's a fool such as I.
Cm
Bb/D
Eb
3
Now and then there's a fool such as
Bb
F
I am over you.
You taught me how to

C7
F
F7
B♭
love, and now you say that we are through. I'm a fool, but I'll
D7
E♭
B♭
love you dear un - til the day I die. Now and then
F7
To Coda
B♭
there's a fool such as I.
D7
E♭
B♭

95

FORTY HOUR WEEK (FOR A LIVIN')

Words and Music by DAVE LOGGINS,
LISA SILVERS and DON SCHLITZ

Moderately ♩ = 80

1. There are people in this country who work hard every day;
not for fame or for-tune do they strive. But the
fruits of their labor are worth more than they're paid And it's

© Copyright 1984 by LEEDS MUSIC CORPORATION, PATCHWORK MUSIC, MUSIC CORPORATION OF AMERICA,
MCA MUSIC PUBLISHING, A Division of MCA INC. and DON SCHLITZ MUSIC, 1755 Broadway, New York, NY 10019
International Copyright Secured   All Rights Reserved

MCA music publishing

time a few of them were rec-og-nized. Hel-lo

Chorus:
De-troit au-to work-er, let me thank you for your time. You work a for-ty hour week for a liv-in' just to send it on down the line. Hel-lo

Pitts-burgh steel mill work-er, let me thank you for your time. You work a for-ty hour week for a liv-in' just to send it on down the line.

Bridge 1:

This is for the one who swings the ham-mer, driv-in' home the nail; for the one be-hind the coun-ter ringin' up the sales; for the one who fights the fire, the one who brings the mail; for everyone who works behind the scenes.

2. You can with the spirit you can't replace with no machine.

Hel-lo A-mer-i-ca, let me thank you for your time.

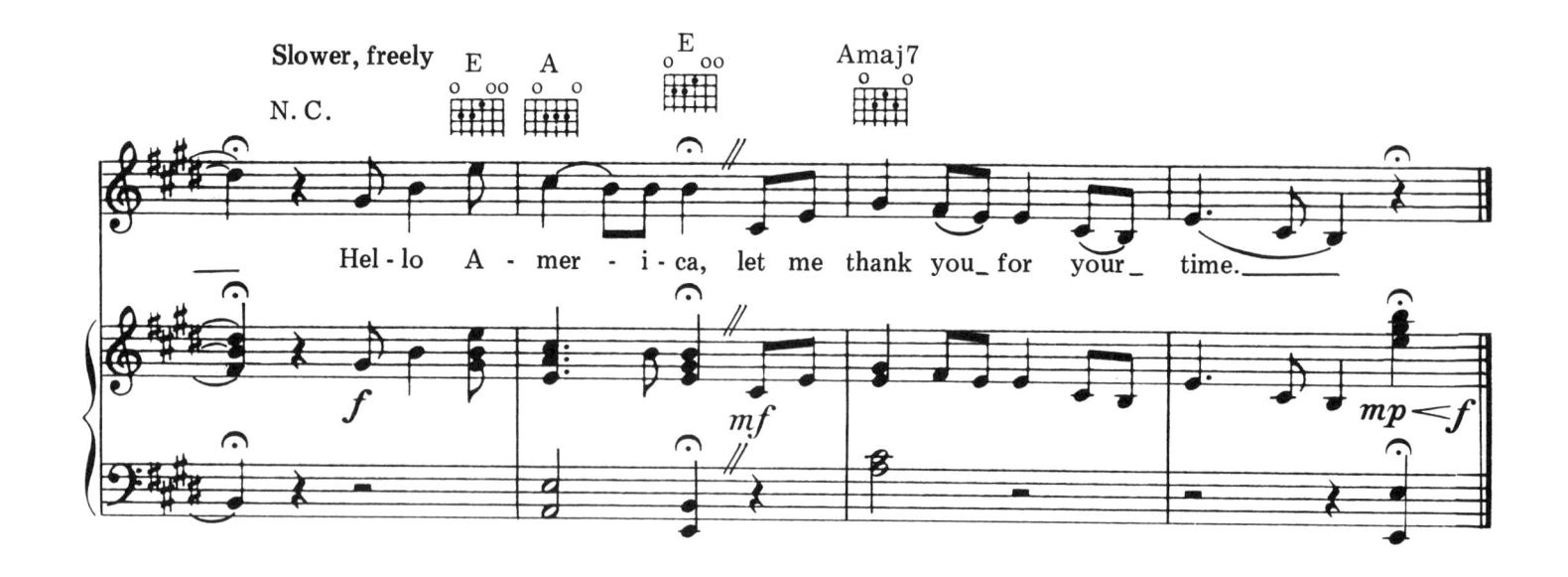

Verse 2:

You can see them every morning
In the factories and the fields,
In the city streets and the quiet country towns.
Workin' together like spokes inside a wheel,
They keep this country turnin' around.

Chorus 2:

Hello Kansas wheatfield farmer,
Let me thank you for your time.
You work a forty hour week for a livin'
Just to send it on down the line.
Hello West Virginia coal miner,
Let me thank you for your time.
You work a forty hour week for a livin'
Just to send it on down the line.

Bridge 2:

This is for the one who drives the big rig
Up and down the road;
For the one out in the warehouse
Bringin' in the load;
For the waitress, the mechanic,
The policeman on patrol;
For everyone who works behind the scenes... *(2nd ending)*

GOLDEN RING

Words and Music by BOBBY BRADDOCK
and RAFE VANHOY

Moderately bright

In a pawn-shop in Chi-ca-go on a sun-ny, sum-mer day, A cou-ple gaz-es at the wed-ding rings there on dis-play. She smiles and nods her

lit-tle wed-ding chap-el lat-er on that af-ter-noon, An old up-right pi-an-o plays that old fa-mil-iar tune. Tears roll down her

small two room a-part-ment, as they fight their fi-nal round, He says, "You won't ad-mit it, but I know you're leav-in' town." She says, "One thing's for

Copyright © 1976 by Tree Publishing Co., Inc.
All Rights Administered by Sony Music Publishing, 8 Music Square West, Nashville, TN 37203
International Copyright Secured   All Rights Reserved

head as he says, "Hon - ey, that's for you. It's not much but it's the
cheeks and hap - py thoughts run through her head, As he whis - pers low, "With
cer - tain, I don't love you an - y - more." And throws down the ring as

best that I can do." Gold - en Ring,
this ring I thee wed." Gold - en Ring,
she walks out the door. Gold - en Ring,

with one ti - ny lit - tle stone, Wait - ing there
with one ti - ny lit - tle stone, Shin - ing ring,
with one ti - ny lit - tle stone, Cast a - side

for some - one to take it home.
now at last it's found a home. By it - self,
like the love that's dead and gone.

it's just a cold me-tal-lic thing, On-ly love can make a gold-en wed-ding ring.

2. In a
3. In a

ring. In a rings there on dis-

play. Gold-en Ring.

HE TALKS TO ME

Words and Music by MIKE REID
and RORY BOURKE

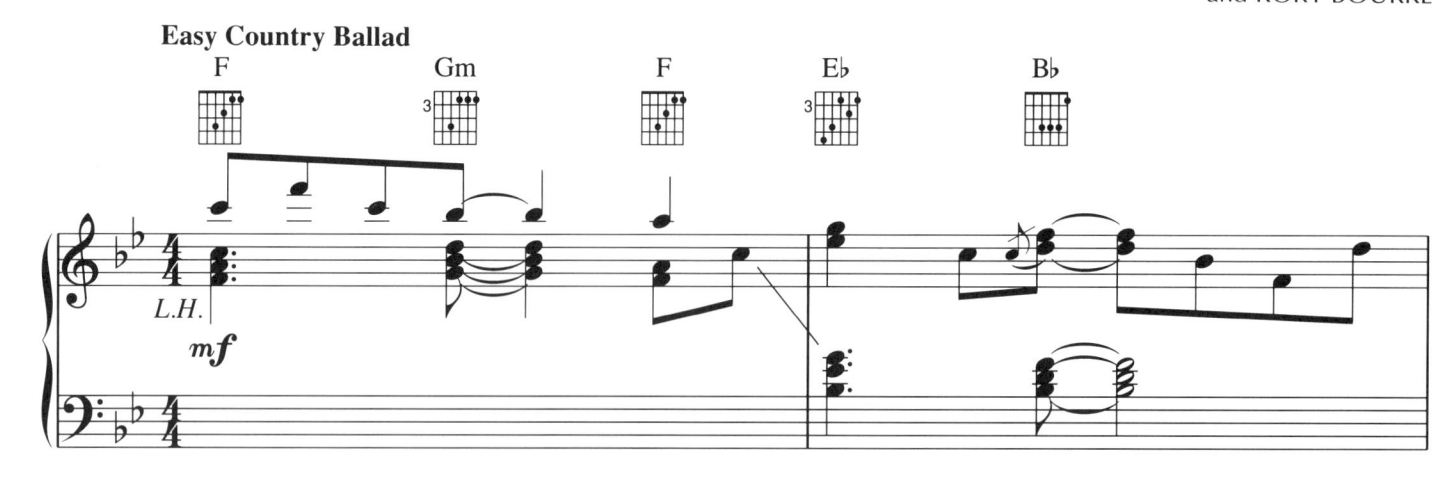

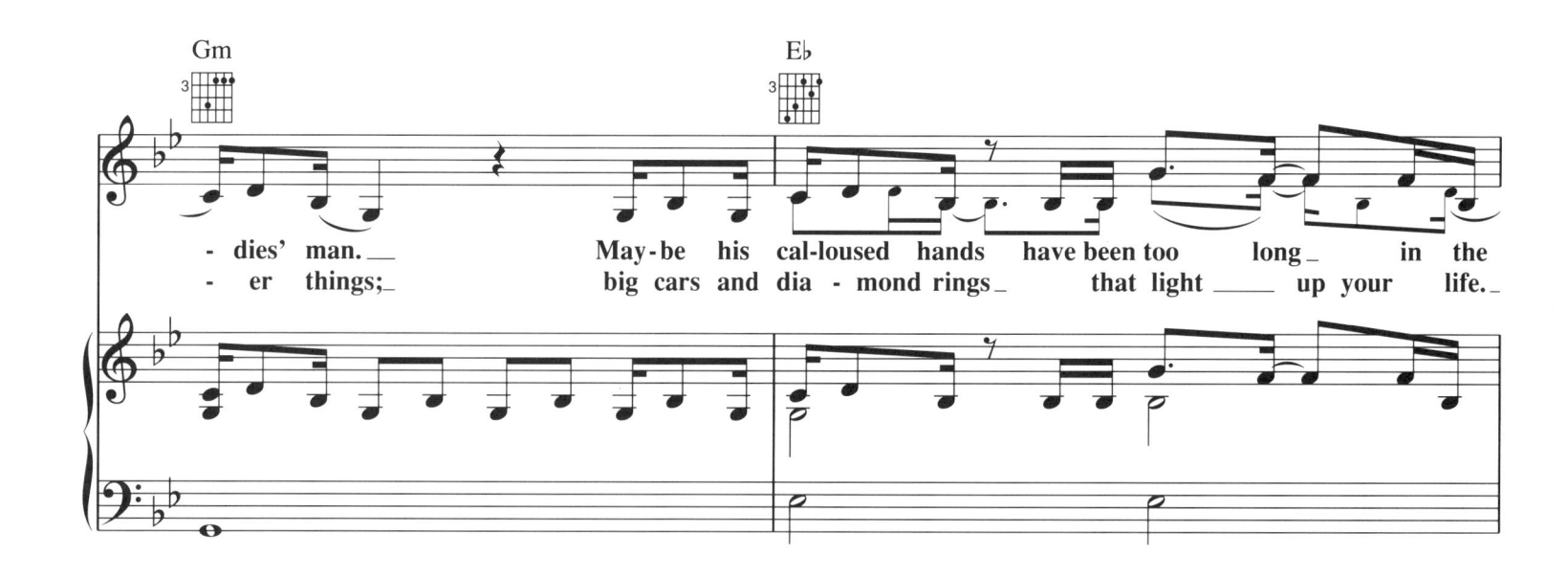

Easy Country Ballad

He may not ev-er be ___ a la-dies' man. ___ May-be his cal-loused hands have been too long ___ in the

Now you can talk a-bout ___ the fin-er things; ___ big cars and dia-mond rings ___ that light ___ up your life.

Copyright © 1985 Lodge Hall Music, Inc., BMG Songs, Inc., RMB Songs and Chappell & Co.
Rights for Lodge Hall Music, Inc. Controlled by BMG Songs, Inc.
Rights for RMB Songs Administered by Chappell & Co.
International Copyright Secured All Rights Reserved

B♭
E♭/B♭
B♭
F7/A
sun.
But he will al-ways be the one
But let me tell you that the
Gm
E♭
I love,
'cause he still does what no one's ev-
fin-est thing
is the joy he brings when we turn out
F7sus
F
Dm
E♭
-er done.
the light.
And it means more to me than
And in those mo-ments
Dm
Csus
C7
he will ev-er know,
'cause words could nev-er say how
af-ter we make love,
that's when he holds me close and gives me

Eb/F F7 Eb Bb
much I love the way he talks to me. It
what I need the most
Dm Gm Bb/F Eb Bb
does my heart good to hear him talk to me.
Cm7 F7sus F7 Eb Bb/D
the way a lov-er should. He can ease my frus-tra-tion with his
D7b9 D7/F# Gm Gm/F Eb Bb/F F7
sooth-in' con-ver-sa-tion. And I love the way he's not a-fraid to

talk to me.

talk to me. Whoa I love the way he's not a-fraid to talk to me.

HERE'S A QUARTER
(CALL SOMEONE WHO CARES)

Words and Music by
TRAVIS TRITT

Rowdy country waltz (♪♪ played as ♩♪)

You say you were wrong to ever leave me alone, and now you're sorry.

You thought what we had could never turn bad, so your leaving You're caught

lone - some ___ and scared. ___
me ___ un a - ware. ___

And you say you'd be ___
But the fact is ___ you've ___

hap - py if you could just ___ come back
run. ___ Girl, ___ that can't ___ be un - done. ___

home. ___ Well, here's a quar - ter. ___ Call ___
So here's a quar - ter. ___ Call ___

someone who cares.
someone who cares.

Call someone who'll listen and might give a damn. Maybe one of your sordid affairs.

But don't you come a-round here handing me none of your lines. Here's a quarter. Call someone who cares.

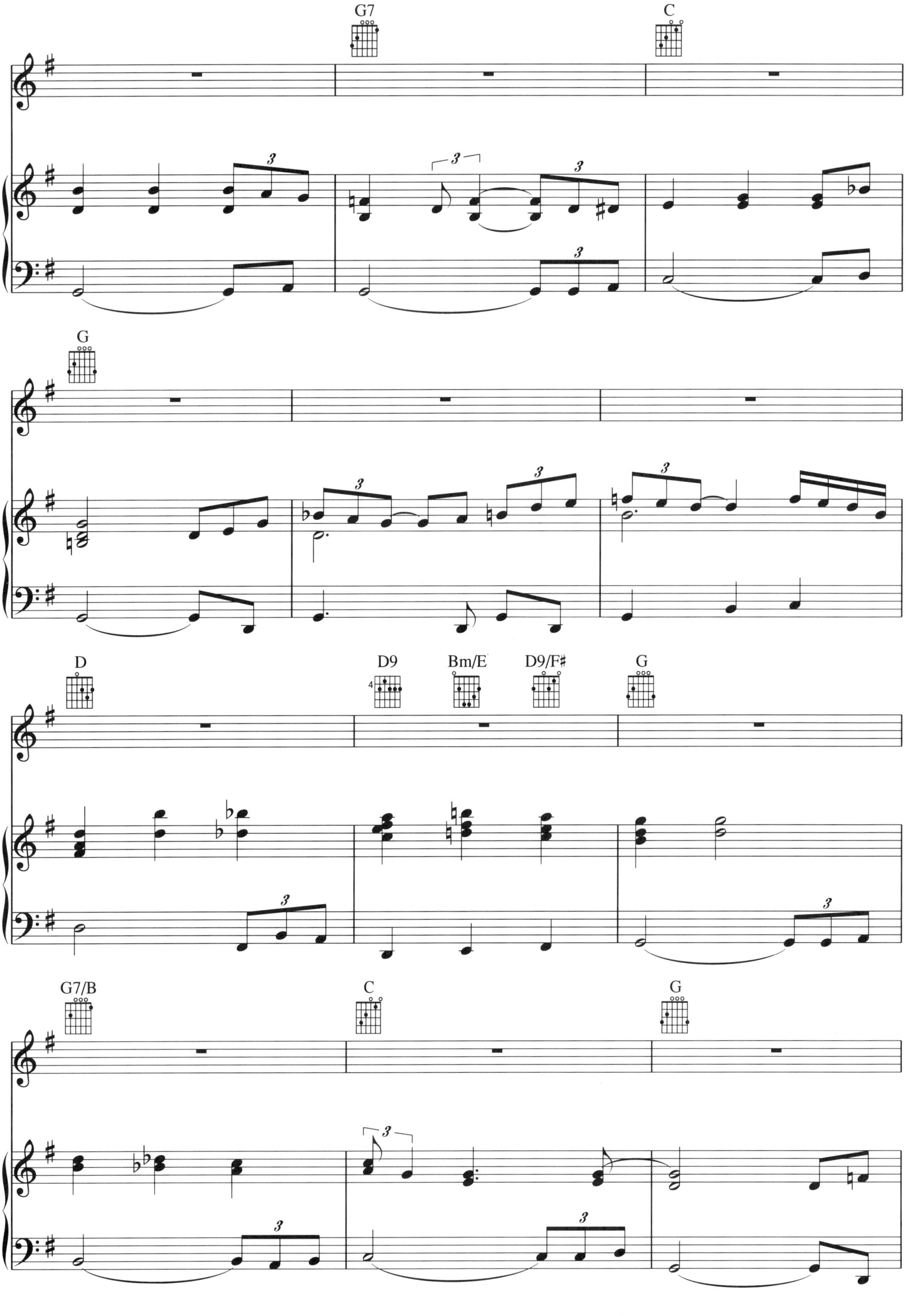
G7
C
G
D
D9
Bm/E
D9/F#
G
G7/B
C
G

113

HOUSTON SOLUTION

Words and Music by DON SCHLITZ
and PAUL OVERSTREET

Easy Country Waltz

I've got some friends down in
dad-dy_____ once

Hous-ton_____
told me_____ who
know me_____ can't
run_____ quite a-

© 1986, 1989 by MCA MUSIC PUBLISHING, A Division of MCA INC., DON SCHLITZ MUSIC, SCREEN GEMS-EMI MUSIC, INC., and SCARLET MOON MUSIC
Rights of DON SCHLITZ MUSIC administered by MCA MUSIC PUBLISHING, A Division of MCA INC., 1755 Broadway, New York, NY 10019
International Copyright Secured All Rights Reserved

well. They'll be more____ than hap-py____ to put me
way. Your trou-bles____ will fol-low____ and

up for____ a spell. I can
find you some - day.____ There's

hang out____ or hide out____ which ev - er____ I
no use____ to ar - gue,____ 'cause he's pro - 'bly

choose, / right. and they won't ask me ques-tions 'bout why / But I've run out of op-tions and I'm

I've got the blues. / leav-in' to-night.

I've got a Hous-ton so-lu-tion in mind. All it

takes is a call on the tel-e-phone / tel-e-phone line, and I / line, And I can / can leave all the prob-lems of Nash-ville be-hind. I've got a

Hous-ton _____ so - lu - tion _____ in mind.

D Em D/F# 2 Em A7
Well my mind. I've got a
G D G
Hous-ton so - lu - tion in mind.
D Em D/F# C/G G C/G G
I've got a Hous - ton so - lu - tion.
rit.

I FEEL LUCKY

Words and Music by MARY-CHAPIN CARPENTER and DON SCHLITZ

Blues Rock

woke up this morning, stumbled out of my rack. I o-
strolled down to the corner, gave my numbers to the clerk. The pot's
lev-en million later, I was sittin' at the bar. I bought

© 1992 EMI APRIL MUSIC INC., GETAREALJOB MUSIC, ALMO MUSIC CORP. and DON SCHLITZ MUSIC
All Rights for GETAREALJOB MUSIC Controlled and Administered by EMI APRIL MUSIC INC.
All Rights Reserved   International Copyright Secured   Used by Permission

-pened up the paper to the page in the back. It on-
— e-lev-en mil-lion, so I called in sick to work. I bought
— the house a dou-ble, then the wait-ress a new car. Dwight

-ly took a min-ute for my fin-ger to find my dail-
— a pack of Cam-els, a bur-rit-o and a Barks, crossed
Yoa-kam's in the cor-ner, try'n to catch my eye. Lyle

-y dose of des-tin-y un-der my sign. My
— a-gainst the light, made a bee-line for the park. The
Lov-ett's right be-side me with his hand up-on my thigh. The

eyes just a-bout popped out-a my head. It said, "The
sky be-gan to thun-der, the wind be-gan to moan. I heard a
mor-al of this sto-ry, it's sim-ple but it's true: hey, the

stars are stacked a-gainst you girl. Get back in bed."
voice a-bove me sayin', "Girl you'd bet-ter get back home." I feel
stars might lie, but the num-bers nev-er do.

luck-y, I feel luck-y, yeah.

No Pro-fes-sor Doom gon-na
No trop-i-cal de-pres-sion gon-na

stand in my way.
steal my sun a-way. Mm, I feel

luck-y to-day.

Well, I

luck-y to-day. *Guitar solo*

B7
F#
D.S. al Coda
Solo ends Now e -
CODA
F#7
Hey Dwight, hey Lyle, boys,
B7
you don't have to fight. Hot dog, I feel
E7
luck - y to - night. I feel luck - y,

125

I MEANT EVERY WORD HE SAID

Words and Music by CURLY PUTMAN,
BUCKY JONES and JOE CHAMBERS

Slow Country Waltz

heard him say ___ "I love you." I heard him say ___ "For-ever," ___ and with-out you he'd rath-er be dead.

I felt my hand shak-ing I felt my heart

Copyright © 1987 Tree Publishing Co., Inc., Cross Keys Publishing Co., Inc., and Joe Chambers Music
All Rights on behalf of Tree Publishing Co., Inc. Administered by Sony Music Publishing, 8 Music Square West, Nashville, TN 37203
All Rights on behalf of Cross Keys Publishing Co., Inc. Administered by Sony Music Publishing, 8 Music Square West, Nashville, TN 37203
International Copyright Secured   All Rights Reserved

breaking ___ 'cause I meant ev-'ry word he ___ said. ___

I saw him whisper something then I
heard him say ___ "I love you." I

saw you look so happy. ___ It's a look I won't
heard him say ___ "For-ev-er." ___ Then he said, "With this

ev-er for-get. ___ 'Cause what-ev-er he
ring I thee wed." ___ And when he said,

told you meant I'd nev-er hold you____ and I meant ev-'ry
"I do," I choked back, "I do, too,"____

word he____ said._____ His heart stole those

words from my head._____ Now it's too late____ to

tell __ you____ what he's al-read-y said.____ I al-read-y

E
B7
said. I heard him say "I love you." I heard him say "For-
F♯m
B
E
ev - er." Then he said, "With this ring I thee wed."
B7
And when he said, "I do," I choked back, "I
F♯m
B7
E
do, too," 'Cause I meant ev -'ry word he said.
rit.

I THOUGHT IT WAS YOU

Words and Music by TIM MENSY
and GARY HARRISON

Moderately

I called your name out loud to a stranger yes-ter-day.
I still drive by your house takin' trips down mem-o-ry lane.

When she turned a-round I said I'm
We had our fu-ture worked out, at least we

Copyright © 1990 Cross Keys Publishing Co., Inc., Miss Dot Music, Inc., Warner-Tamerlane Publishing Corp. and Patrick Joseph Music, Inc.
All Rights on behalf of Cross Keys Publishing Co., Inc. and Miss Dot Music, Inc. administered by Sony Music Publishing, 8 Music Square West, Nashville, TN 37203
International Copyright Secured   All Rights Reserved

sor - ry and just walked a - way.
did on that old porch swing.

From a dis - tance she had that look
To - day in my rear - view mir - ror

and for a sec - ond or two
I saw an old Mal - i - bu

I thought it was you.
girl, I thought it was you. It took a mo -

-ment to catch my breath, tried to brace myself. Still don't have a clue how to leave your mem-'ry behind after all this time. I hear there's one special love in each life and I must look like a fool. I thought it was you.

Am I real-ly a fool? I thought it was you.

I thought it was you.

Why could-n't it be you?

Repeat and Fade

I WON'T TAKE LESS THAN YOUR LOVE

Words and Music by DON SCHLITZ
and PAUL OVERSTREET

Moderately bright country

"How much do I owe you," said the husband to his wife,
"How much do I owe you," said the man to his Lord,
"for standing beside me through the hard years of my life?
"for giving me this day and ev'ry day that's gone before?
Shall I bring you
Shall I build you a tem-

© Copyright 1987, 1988 by MCA MUSIC PUBLISHING, A Division of MCA INC., DON SCHLITZ MUSIC, WRITERS GROUP MUSIC and SCARLET MOON MUSIC
Rights of DON SCHLITZ MUSIC administered by MCA MUSIC PUBLISHING, A Division of MCA INC., 1755 Broadway, New York, NY 10019
International Copyright Secured   All Rights Reserved

dia - monds? Shall I buy you furs?
- ple? Shall I make a sac - ri - fice?
B♭ C B♭
Say the word and it's yours."
Tell me Lord, and I will pay the price."
C F
And his wife said, "I won't take less than your love, sweet
And the Lord said, "I won't take less than your love, sweet
B♭ F
love. No, I won't take less than your love.
love. No, I won't take less than your love.

All the rich-es of the world could nev-er be e-nough, and I won't take less than your love."

All the trea-sures of the world could nev-er be e-nough, and I

"How much do I owe, you," to the

mother said the son, "for all that you have taught me in the days when I was young? Shall I bring expensive blankets to cast upon your bed, And a pillow for to rest your weary head?" And the mother said, "I won't take less than your love, sweet love. No, I won't take less than your love. All the comforts of the world could never be enough, and I won't take less than your love."

Am
G
F
Am
G
F
D.S. al Coda
CODA
B♭
C
F
won't take less. I won't take less than your
love sweet love. No, I won't take less than your
B♭

love. All the trea-sures of the world could nev-er be e-nough. And I won't take less than your love. No, I won't take less than your love."

IF THE DEVIL DANCED (IN EMPTY POCKETS)

Words and Music by KIM WILLIAMS
and KEN SPOONER

Moderate country two-beat

C7
got a - round, no mon - ey down, take
own a home, I've got a loan,
A7
D
years and years to pay. When I
tai - lor made for you. Then a -
C7
got there, the lot was bare, but the
bove the rack - et a voice in my jack - et said,
G
C7
C♯dim
sales - man said hold on. For a lit - tle cash, I got - ta
"I'll tote the note." The de - vil made me do it, talked

G/D B7/D♯ E A7 D7
two - tone Nash out be - hind the barn.
me in - to it, and that was all she wrote.
G
Solo ends If the de - vil danced in emp - ty pock - ets,
A7 D
he'd have a ball in mine. With a nine foot grand, a
G6 G♯dim Am D
ten piece band and a twelve girl chor - us line. I'd raise

some loot in a three piece suit, give 'em one dance for a dime. If the de-vil danced in emp-ty pock-ets, he'd have a ball in mine. Well They say debt is a bot-tom-less pit where the de-vil likes to play.

I'd sell my soul to get out of this hole, but there'd be hell to pay.

IN A DIFFERENT LIGHT

Words and Music by BUCKY JONES, BOB McDILL and DICKEY LEE

Moderately slow

Ev-'ry morn-ing I watch you walk in-to the of-fice in your bus-'ness suit and match-ing shoes. With your hair pulled up neat-ly, you

girls at the of-fice walk the guys al-ways no-tice when they walk by, but you're not the type. Oh, they don't know what I know 'cause

Copyright © 1986 Cross Keys Publishing Co., Inc., PolyGram International Publishing, Inc., Ranger Bob Music and Songs Of PolyGram International, Inc.
All Rights on behalf of Cross Keys Publishing Co., Inc. administered by Sony Music Publishing, 8 Music Square West, Nashville, TN 37203
International Copyright Secured All Rights Reserved

tug at your glass-es   and you sit down just
some things just don't show through tail-ored tweeds and that's

three desks down. And I watch you in the fluo-res-cent glare
fine with me. Let them all think what they want to.

and my mind drifts a-way some-where.
As for me when I look at you

And I see you in a

dif-f'rent light, your hair falling down with love in your eyes. In my mind you're a beau-ti-ful sight. I see you in a dif-f'rent light just the way I saw you last night.

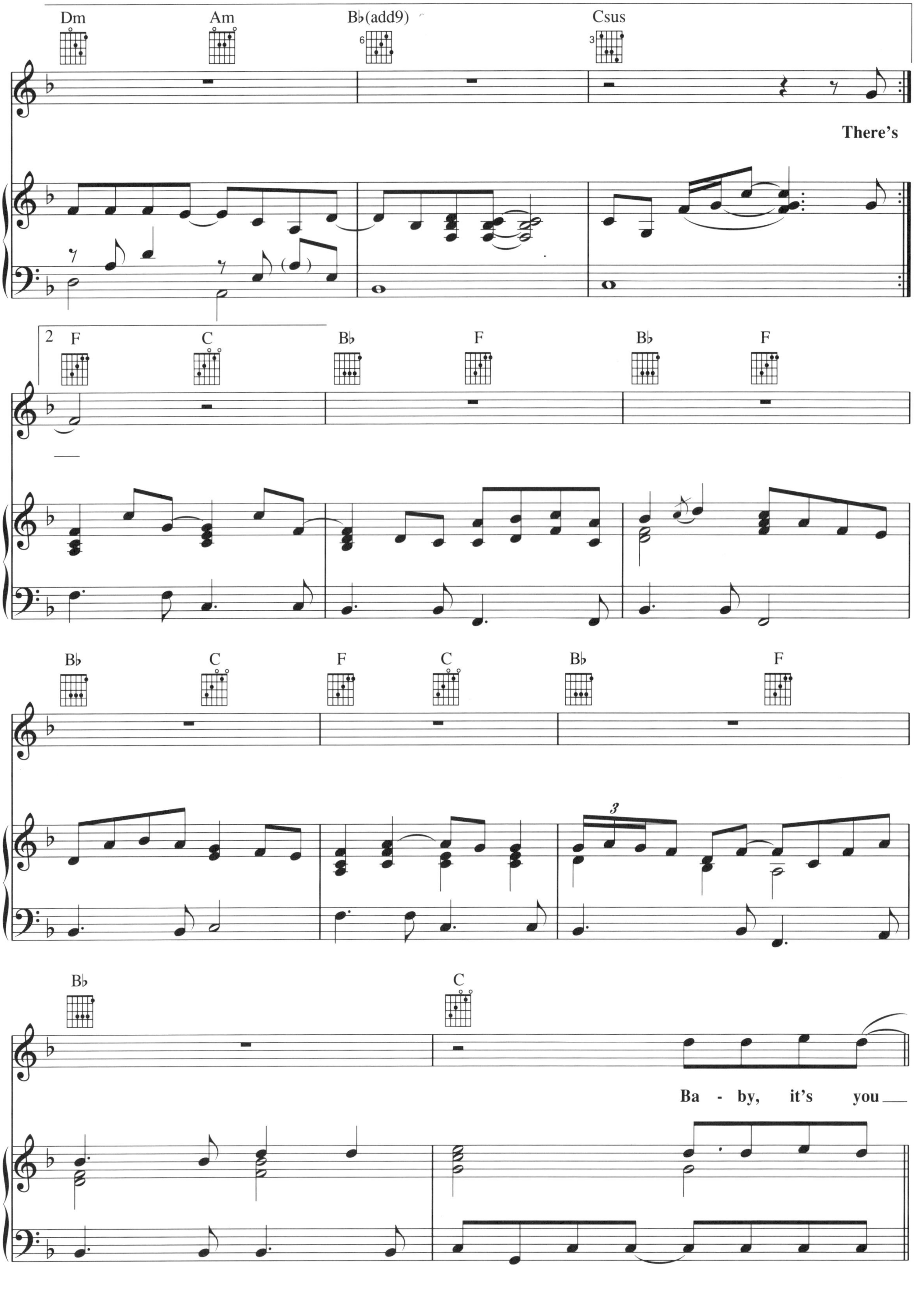
Dm
Am
B♭(add9)
Csus
There's
2
F
C
B♭
F
B♭
F
B♭
C
F
C
B♭
F
3
B♭
C
Ba - by, it's you

F C B♭ F
It's you in a dif - f'rent light, your hair
B♭ F B♭ C
fall - ing down with love in your eyes. In my
F C B♭ F B♭ F/A
mind you're a beau - ti - ful sight. I see you in a dif - f'rent light
Gm7 B♭ C
Repeat and Fade
just the way I saw you last night.

IS IT RAINING AT YOUR HOUSE

Words and Music by HANK COCHRAN,
DEAN DILLON and VERN GOSDIN

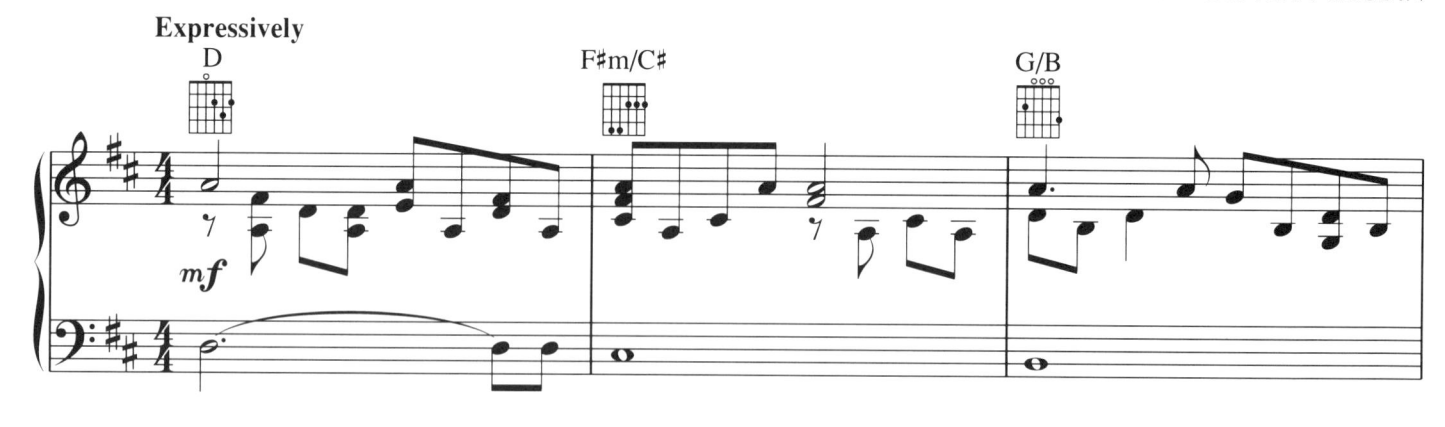

Is __ it rain - ing __ at your house
rain - ing __ at your place

like it's rain - ing _____ at mine? __
just like it is _____ o - ver here? __

Copyright © 1986 Tree Publishing Co., Inc., Jesse Jo Music, MCA Music Publishing, A Division of MCA Inc. and Hookem Music
All Rights on behalf of Tree Publishing Co., Inc. administered by Sony Music Publishing, 8 Music Square West, Nashville, TN 37203
Rights for Jesse Jo Music Administered by MCA Music Publishing, A Division of MCA Inc., 1755 Broadway, New York, NY 10019
International Copyright Secured   All Rights Reserved
MCA music publishing

F♯m/C♯
Do you miss me like I miss you?
If it is, then sweet-heart,
G/B
A
Is it cloud-y all the time?
like me I know you're scared.
D
F♯m/C♯
Do you trem-ble when the phone rings
I just called you to con-sole you
G/B
Gm6/B♭
and you think I'm on the line? Is it
like an-y old friend would do.

(Sheet music page 154)

Lyrics:
rain-ing __ Is it rain-ing __ at your house? __ at your house? __ like it's rain-ing at mine? __ Does it thun-der and __ light-ning ev - en when the sun __ shines? __ Is it rain-ing __ at your house __

like it's rain-ing at mine?

Is it

And by the way, I still love you.

IT AIN'T NOTHIN'

Words and Music
by TONY HASELDEN

Easy, with a bounce

My boss_ is the boss_
It was writ-ten all _

-'s son,_ and that makes_ for a real_ long day._
o-ver her face_ she was a-bout_ to climb_ the walls._

When that day is fin-al-ly done_ I'm fac-ing
She said, "You got-ta get me out-a this place,_ 'cause e-ven

Copyright © 1989 by Millhouse Music
All Rights managed worldwide by Songs Of PolyGram International, Inc.
International Copyright Secured   All Rights Reserved

B7
E7
E♭9
for - ty thou - sand cars on the in - ter - state.
Cin - der - el - la got to go to the ball."
D9
D7
A13
G13
Feel - in' low - er than a well - dig - ger's shoes, knee deep in a
If you mul - ti - ply hell times three that's what this day's been
F♯13
B7
mess of blues. But those blues just fade a - way when I
like for me. I said hon - ey we'll do the town, just
E7
E7/G♯
A
A♯dim
hear my ba - by say
don't let it get you down. 'cause
it ain't noth - in' a
Instrumental ends

lit - tle bit of love won't fix. It ain't noth - in' but a scratch, a lit - tle bit of love can stitch. It ain't noth - in' a lit - tle bit of love can't heal. Your love makes me feel, no mat - ter what hand life deals

159

KEEP IT BETWEEN THE LINES

Words and Music by RUSSELL SMITH
and KATHY LOUVIN

Moderate four-beat

He was
sit - tin' be - side___ me in the pas - sen - ger seat as I
sit - tin' in my chair,___ kind - a sneak - in' a look at him
fin - ished the pic - ture and I put him to bed. Got

looked through the wind - shield at the qui - et lit - tle street. He was
ly - in' on the floor___ with his col - or - ing book. Then he
down on my knees___ and I bowed my head. And I said,

© Copyright 1991 by MCA MUSIC PUBLISHING, A Division of MCA INC., 1755 Broadway, New York, NY 10019 and TILLIS TUNES, INC.
International Copyright Secured   All Rights Reserved
MCA music publishing

smil - ing, so proud as he gave me the key. But
caught me watch - in' and he climbed on my knee. Said,
"Fa - ther, oh Fa - ther, I feel so a - lone. Are you

in - side I knew he was as nerv - ous as me. And I said,
"Dad - dy, oh Dad - dy, would you do one with me?" Then I
sure I can raise him with his mom - my gone?" Then the

"Dad - dy, oh Dad - dy, are you sure I know how? Are you
hugged him so tight - ly as we turned the page. Said, "I
an - swer came back, so gen - tle and low in the

sure that I'm read-y __ to drive __ this car now?" He said, "I'm
have-n't done this since I was your age." He said, "I'm
words of my dad-dy __ from so __ long a-go. Said, "I'm

right here be-side __ you, and you're gon-na do fine.
right here be-side __ you, and you're gon-na do fine. Dad-dy,
right here be-side __ you, and you're gon-na do fine.

All you got-ta do is keep it be-tween __ the lines."
all you got-ta do is keep it be-tween __ the lines."
All you got-ta do is keep it be-tween __ the lines."

Gm F/A B♭ C7 F
'Cause it's a long, nar - row road.
B♭ C Dm
On - ly the good Lord knows where it leads in the
B♭ F/A Gm B♭/F C Gm/D
end, but you got to be - gin.
C/E B♭ C F
So keep your hands on the wheel. Be -

lieve in the things__ that are real.__ Just take__ your__ time and keep it be-tween__ the lines.__

I was __ So we

CODA

So keep your hands on the wheel.__

Believe in the things that are real.

Take your time and keep it between the lines.

Just take your time and keep it between the lines.

LIFE'S TOO LONG
(To Live Like This)

Words and Music by DAN WILSON,
DON COOK and JOHN JARVIS

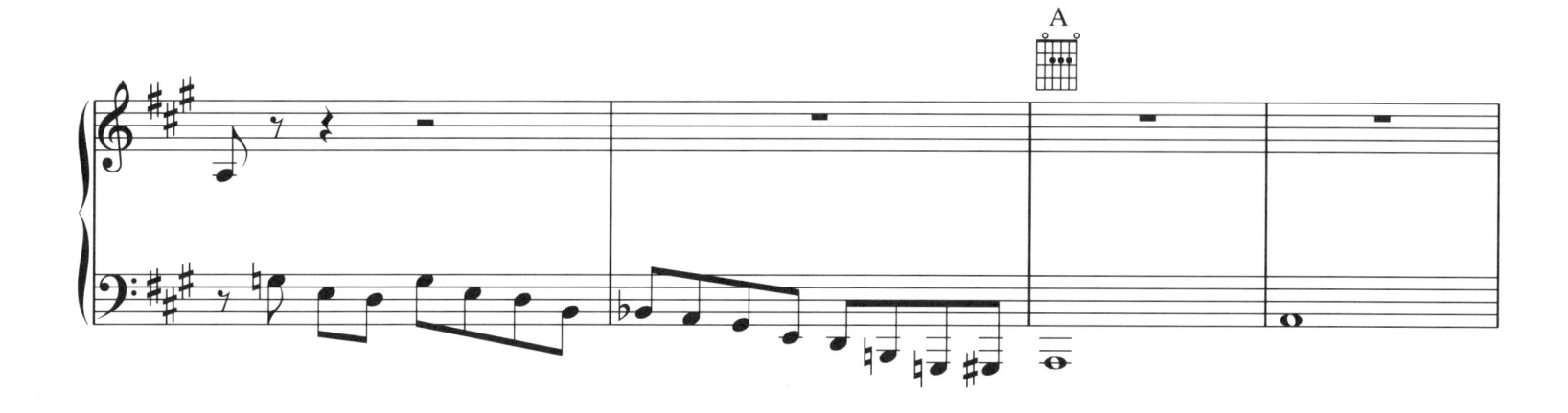

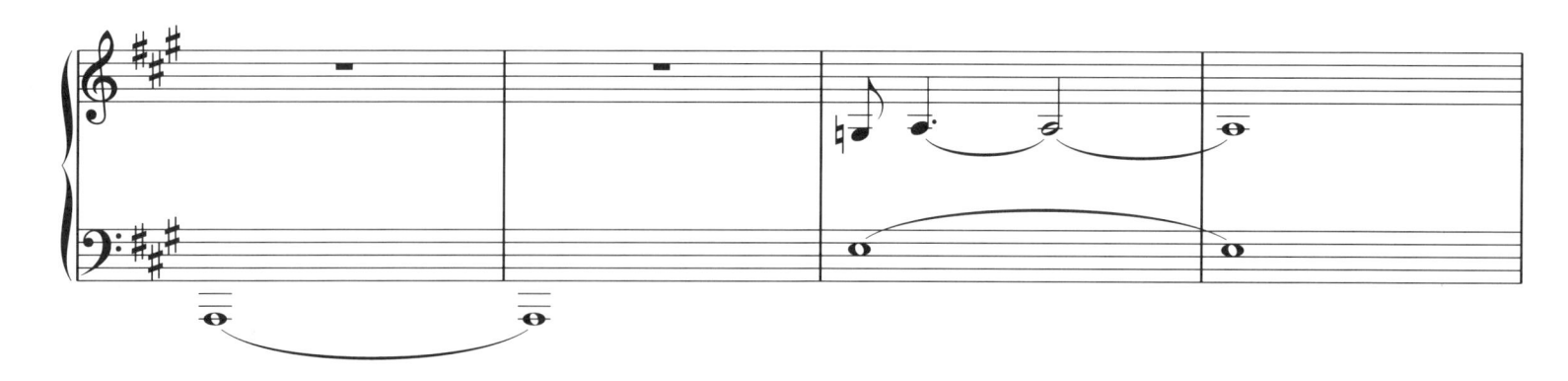

Fast Country two-beat

A G
Drive - time traf - fic in the
Mail - box fill - ing up with
Ain't no fu - ture in this
D A G
pour - ing rain. Six car pile up in the
bills to pay. Boss man hang - ing on my
T. V. Guide. Ain't no rea - son we should
D E A G
pass - ing lane. Can't help think - ing while I
back all day. Gon - na work me to the
stay in - side. Some - one's hav - ing all the
D A
To Coda
shake my fist,
bone, I guess.
fun we miss.
Life's too long to

live like this." this."

Come here, baby. Give your man a hug. All we've got that they can't take is love. Let 'em roll. We ain't got much to lose but these stay-put, stay-home, way too a-lone blues.

Instrumental solo

To Coda II ⊕ ⊕
A
D
E+
A
D.S. al Coda
Solo ends
CODA
no chord
Life's too long to
live like this.
A
D.S.S. al Coda II
CODA II
A
Solo ends
E7

171

Life's too long, yeah,
Life's too

life's too long.

Come on, baby. Give your man a kiss.

Life's too long to live like this.

Repeat and Fade

LOVE WILL FIND ITS WAY TO YOU

Bright shuffle (♪♪ played as ♩♪)

Words and Music by DAVE LOGGINS
and J.D. MARTIN

An-oth-er morn-ing, an-oth-er day in your life
An-oth-er par-ty and all your friends are smiles.

with-out some-one there by you.
Oh, you might meet some-one new.

© Copyright 1984 by MCA MUSIC PUBLISHING, A Division of MCA INC. and PATCHWORK MUSIC
Rights of PATCHWORK MUSIC administered by MCA MUSIC PUBLISHING, A Division of MCA INC., 1755 Broadway, New York, NY 10019
International Copyright Secured   All Rights Reserved

You had a dream a-gain last night.
Be-in' close would be so nice.

You won-der why the dream just won't come true.
In this life the chan-ces are so few. So

what 'cha gon-na do? Walk a-round with your head hung down.

Ba-by, that's the rea-son you've nev-er found the

B7/D♯ Dm7 F/G
one for you. So you got to let your love shine
C G/C C G/C
through your eyes, your smile.
F C/G G F/G G
You've got to let some - bod - y know how you feel in - side
C G/C C G/C
your heart, you'll find.

F
C/G
F/G
C/G
G
To Coda
Some - bod - y wants to be a part of your life.
F
C/E
F
And if you'll just be - lieve and say that's what you're gon - na do,
C/E
Cm/E♭
Dm
C/E
F
F/G
one day love will find its way to you.
C
G/C
C
G/C
Yes, it will.

Dm
C/E
1
F
F/G
One day love will find its way to you.
C
G/C
C
G/C
F
C/G
F/G
C/G
G
2
F
F/G
Fmaj9
find its way to you.
G/F
F
Don't you ev - er think you're the on - ly one.

G/F
Fmaj9
Em
Am
3
Oh, some - where in the world there's a
Dm
Em
F
F/G
A
lone - ly heart look - in' for some - one.
E/A
Em7/A
Dm7
F/G
D.S. al Coda
You've got to let your love shine
CODA
C
G/C
C
G/C
'Cause your eyes, your smile,

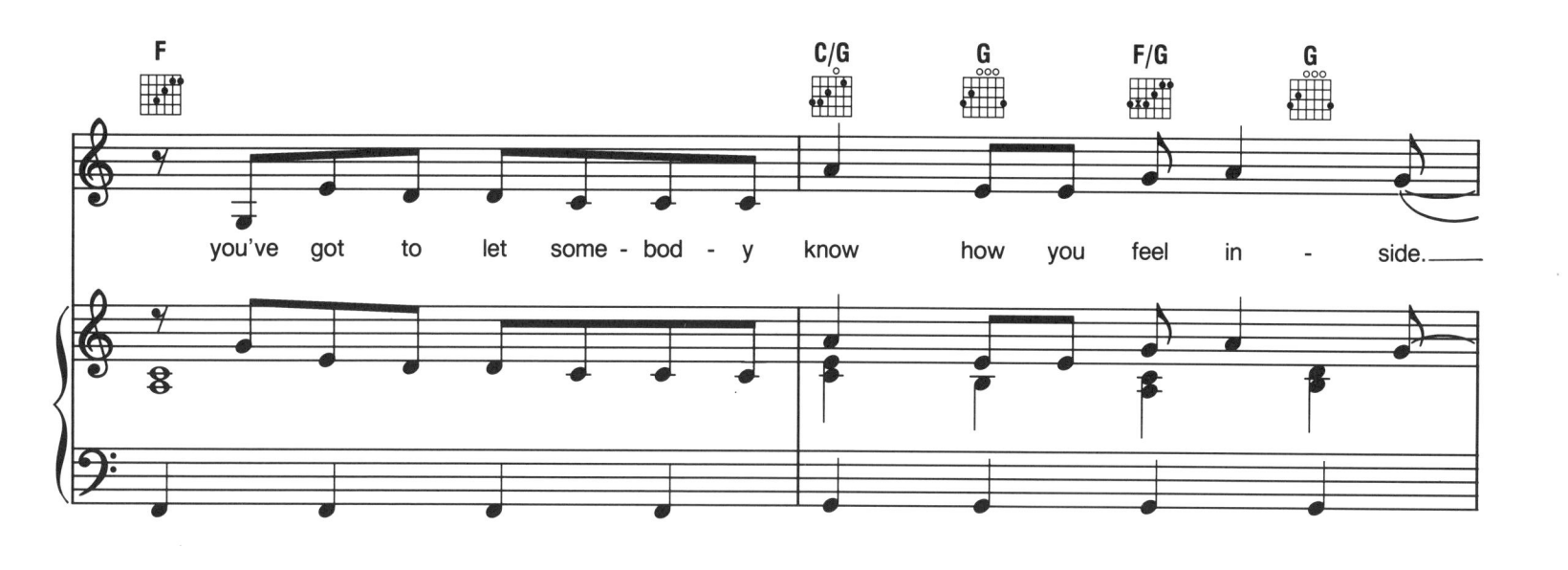

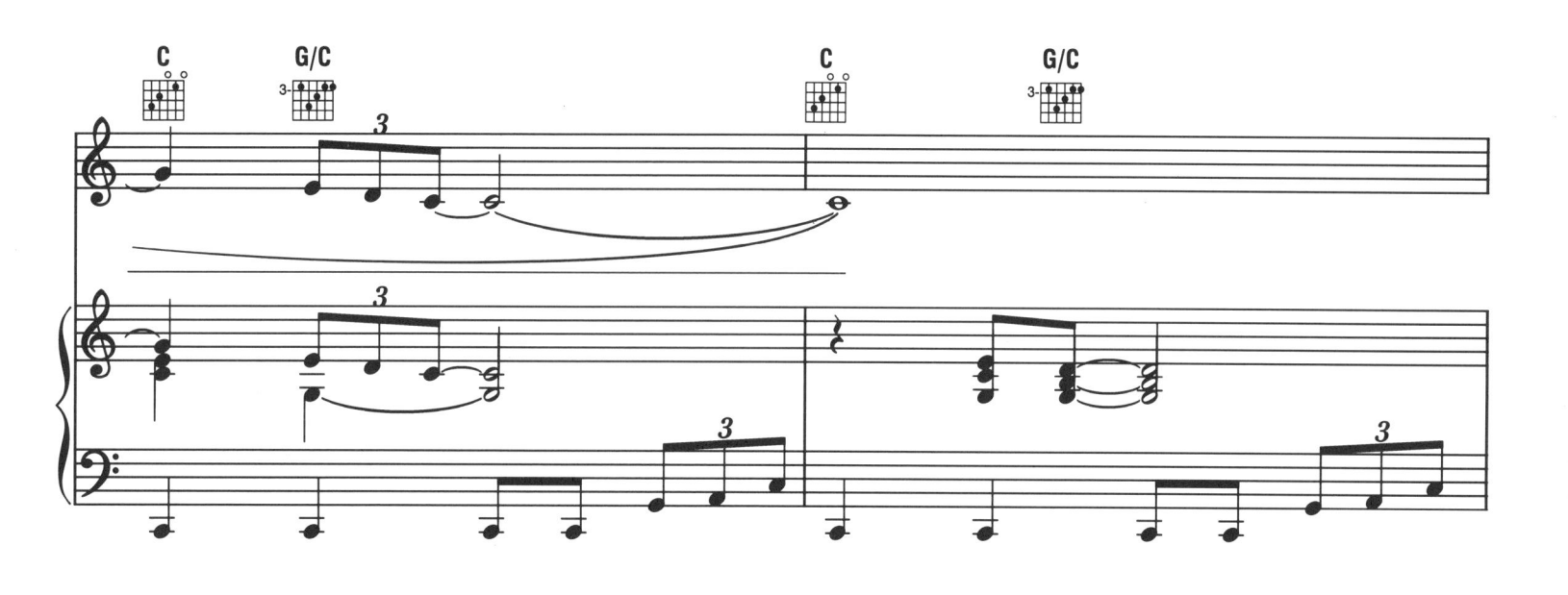

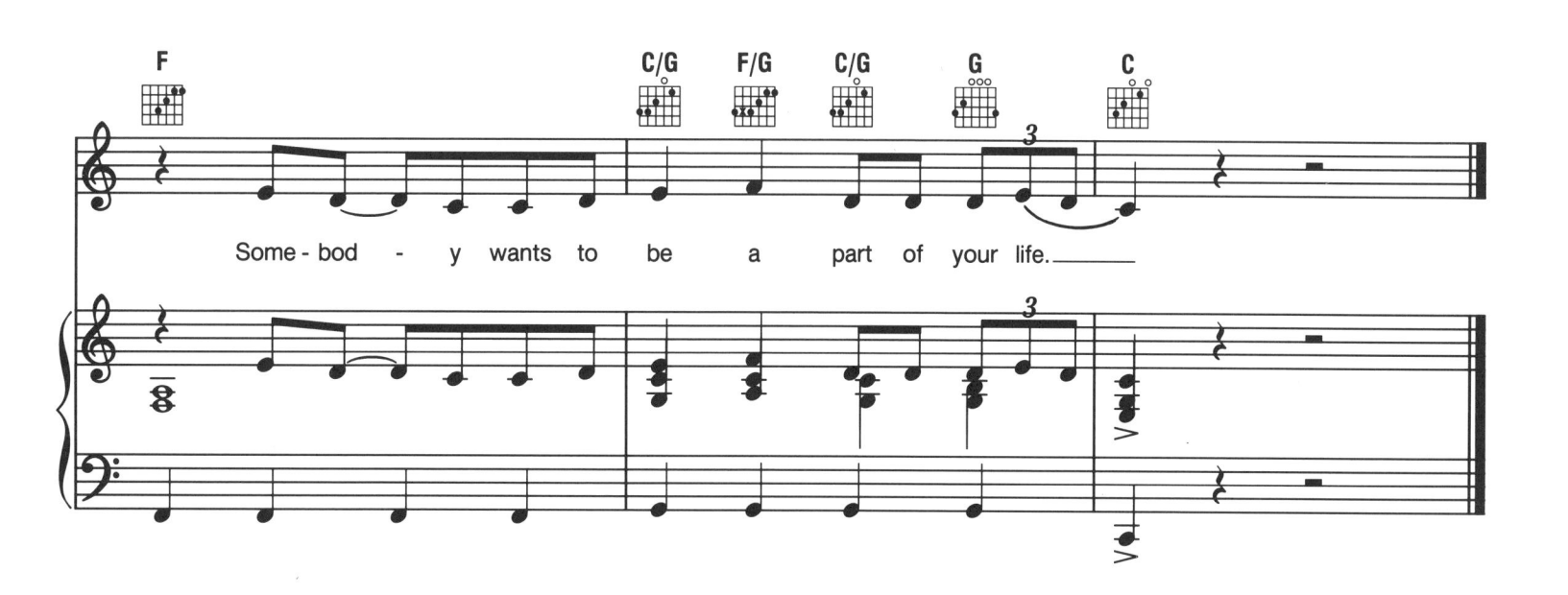

you've got to let some-bod-y know how you feel in-side.

Some-bod-y wants to be a part of your life.

MAMA TRIED

Words and Music by
MERLE HAGGARD

The first thing I remember knowin' was a lonesome whistle blowin', And a young-on's dream of growin' up to ride, on a freight train leavin' town, not knowin' where I'm bound, And no one could change my mind, but Mama tried. One and only rebel child, from a fam'ly meek and

daddy, rest his soul, left my mom a heavy

G D G A7 D G
mild, My ma-ma seemed to know what lay in store, 'Spite of all my Sun-day learn-in' towards the
load, She tried so ver-y hard to fill his shoes, Work-in' hou-rs with-out rest, want-ed
D G D A7 D
bad I kept on turn-in', 'Til ma-ma could-n't hold me an-y-more.
me to have the best, She tried to raise me right but I re-fused.
And I turned
G D G D
twen-ty one in pris-on do-in' life with-out pa-role, No one could steer me right, but ma-ma
A7 D G D
tried, ma-ma tried. Ma-ma tried to raise me bet-ter, but her plead-ing I de-nied, That leaves
A7 1. D 2. D
on-ly me to blame, 'cause ma-ma tried. Dear ol' tried.

MIRROR MIRROR

Words and Music by
MARK SANDERS,
JOHN JARRARD and BOB DiPIERO

© Copyright 1991 by MCA MUSIC PUBLISHING, A Division of MCA INC., 1755 Broadway, New York, NY 10019,
ALABAMA BAND MUSIC, LITTLE BIG TOWN MUSIC and AMERICAN MADE MUSIC
International Copyright Secured   All Rights Reserved

MCA music publishing

who is the lone - li - est fool of all. Now, wait a min - ute, I be - lieve I see the an - swer star - ing back at me.

G(no3rd)
To Coda
C
Spent most of the morn - ing
Yes, I'm one who swore
G
lay - ing in bed.
she would stay,
Lunch was black
right up to the mo -
cof - fee and three cig - a - rettes.
- ment the U - Haul drove a - way.
They
She

say it'll kill me, but I've got a hunch
did-n't leave a ta-ble, she did-n't leave a chair,

that this brok-en heart's gon-na
but she knew what she was do-in' when she left

beat them to the punch. Oh,
you hang in' there. Oh,

CODA

Now, wait one min-ute, I believe I see the an-swer star-ing back at me.

MY NEXT BROKEN HEART

Words and Music by DON COOK,
RONNIE DUNN and KIX BROOKS

| G |

stepping out _____ all o- ver town. _____
taught me how _____ to hurt _____ so well, _____

| C |

| G |

Drove me back to drink - ing _____ in _____ this
When it comes to love _____ I _____ know _____ my

| D7 |

bar. _____
part. _____

| G |

Well, I found_ my-self_ a brand_
And I'll play_ this game_ that I_

_____ new friend. I'm head-ed down _____ that road _____
_____ can't win. I'll be some-bod - y's fool _____

| G |

a - gain.
a - gain. } I'm working on my next broken heart.

Solo ends I thought all a - long you'd be the death of me, but I've met one, to - night, who wants what's left of me. ____ I've seen ____ that look ____ be-fore. ____ She'll tear ____ my world ____ a-part. ____ I'm work-ing on ____ my next bro-ken heart. ____

CODA
G
C
I'm
G
D
G
working on my next broken heart.
C
G
Woh I'm working on my
D
G
next broken heart.

MY ARMS STAY OPEN ALL NIGHT

Words and Music by DON SCHLITZ
and PAUL OVERSTREET

Moderate Country two beat

I know you like the nightlife, the parties and the fun.
Please don't think I'm crazy, I haven't lost my mind.
You like to hang around until the last song has been sung.
But when it comes to loving you I can always find the time.
So I have made arrangements.
So if it's after mid-

© Copyright 1989 by MCA MUSIC PUBLISHING, A Division of MCA INC., DON SCHLITZ MUSIC, SCREEN GEMS-EMI MUSIC, INC. and SCARLET MOON MUSIC
Rights of DON SCHLITZ MUSIC administered by MCA MUSIC PUBLISHING, A Division of MCA INC., 1755 Broadway, New York, NY 10019
International Copyright Secured   All Rights Reserved

MCA music publishing

-ments, and I wanted you to know
-night or just before the break of day,

when all the laughter's ended there's still somewhere you can go.
anytime you need me it'll never be too late.

'Cause {My/my} arms stay open all night,

from sundown 'til the morning light, hoping you can find

_____ where you _____ be-long. _____ I leave the lights _____ on. _____
My heart is nev-er closed. _____ You're the on - ly _____
love it knows. _____ The one dream _____ I have _____ is to hold _____ you tight. _____
My arms stay o-pen all _____ night. _____

C(add9) D G D(add11) C D
Oh, yeah.
Em C Em
When all your so-called friends go home, you don't ev - er have to
3
Dsus D
D.S. al Coda
be a - lone 'cause
CODA
C(add9) D G D(add11) C(add9) D
Ooh.
G D C Dsus D G D C(add9) D
Repeat and Fade
My arms stay o - pen all night.

ONE PROMISE TOO LATE

Words and Music by DAVE LOGGINS,
DON SCHLITZ and LISA SILVER

Moderately (In 2)

I would've waited for ev-
But I met some-one be-fore

F
C
- er
___ you
if I'd
and my
G
Am
known that you'd ___ be here. ___
heart just could - n't wait. ___
F
C
We could - 've shared ___ our lives to - geth -
so no mat - ter how ___ much I a - dore ___
G
Dm
- er ___
___ you, ___
and held each
I've got to

F
1 Gsus
G
oth - er close all through the years.
stand be - hind the
2 Gsus
G
no chord
pro - mise that I made. Where were
Am
F
you when I could - 've loved
C
you? Where were

Am
F
you when I gave my heart a-
Gsus
G
F
way? All my life I've
G
Am
F
been dream-ing of you. You came a-long
C
G
Am
one pro-mise too late.

F
C
G
To Coda
You came a - long one pro - mise too late.
1 C
To next strain
2 C
late.
3
D.S. al Coda
Em
Where were
I won't say that I'm sor - ry that I met you.
Am
Em
I can't have

you but I nev - er will for - get you. Where were

late.

ONLY HERE FOR A LITTLE WHILE

Words and Music by WAYLAND HOLYFIELD
and RICHARD LEIGH

Moderate Country two-beat

I'm gon-na hold who needs hold-in', mend what needs mend-in', walk what needs walk-in', though it means an ex-tra mile.

© 1990 EMI APRIL MUSIC INC., IDES OF MARCH MUSIC and LION-HEARTED MUSIC
All Rights Controlled and Administered by EMI APRIL MUSIC INC.
All Rights Reserved International Copyright Secured Used by Permission

Pray what needs pray - in', say what needs say - in', 'cause we're on - ly here for a lit - tle while.

To - day, I stood sing - in' songs
stop and think, "What's the hur -

G
D
and say - in' "A - men," say - in'
- ry? Why the run - nin'?" I don't
G
D
"Good - bye" to an old friend who
like what I'm be - com - in'. Gon - na
E7
A
D
G
seemed so young. Well, he spent his life
change my style, take my time
D
G
work - in' hard to chase a dol -
and not take it all for grant -

-lar,___ puttin' off un - til ___ to - mor-
-ed ___ 'cause we're

-row ___ things he should have ___ done.

It made me on - ly here ___ for a lit - tle while. ___

D.S. al Coda

Gon - na

CODA
D
E
Let me love
like I'll never see tomorrow, treat each
A
E
day as though it's borrowed, like it's precious as a child.
F#
B
Whoa, take my hand,

let us reach out to each oth-er 'cause we're on-ly here for a lit-tle while. Gon-na hold who needs hold-in', mend what needs mend-in', walk what needs walk - in', __ though it means an ex - tra mile. __

Pray what __ needs pray - in', __ say __ what __ needs say - in' __ 'cause we're on - ly here for a lit - tle while. __

Gon - na

RUMOR HAS IT

Words and Music by LARRY SHELL,
VERN DANT and BRUCE BURCH

D
A
bout __ us, on - ly her a - gain. ___
gos - sip when there's noth-ing else to say. ___
E
A
E
I ________ did - n't wan - na
I ________ would - n't have ________
A
Em7
A7
lis - ten, but I ______ hung on ev - 'ry _____
be - lieved _ my ears, but I see ______ it __ in __________ your ____
D
___ word. __ They said some __ things ___ I ____
___ eyes. __ Those sto - ries ___ go - in' ___

A
E
A
wish I had - n't heard.
round this town aren't lies.
3
3
3
E
Oh, ru - mor has it she has
A
F♯m7
you. Ru - mor has it
B
A/B
E
A
that you love her, too. Oh, the

D
E
talk is cheap, but the price is high when it's
F#m7
D
true. Oh, ru - mor
A
E7
1A
has it she has you.
D
A
D
This

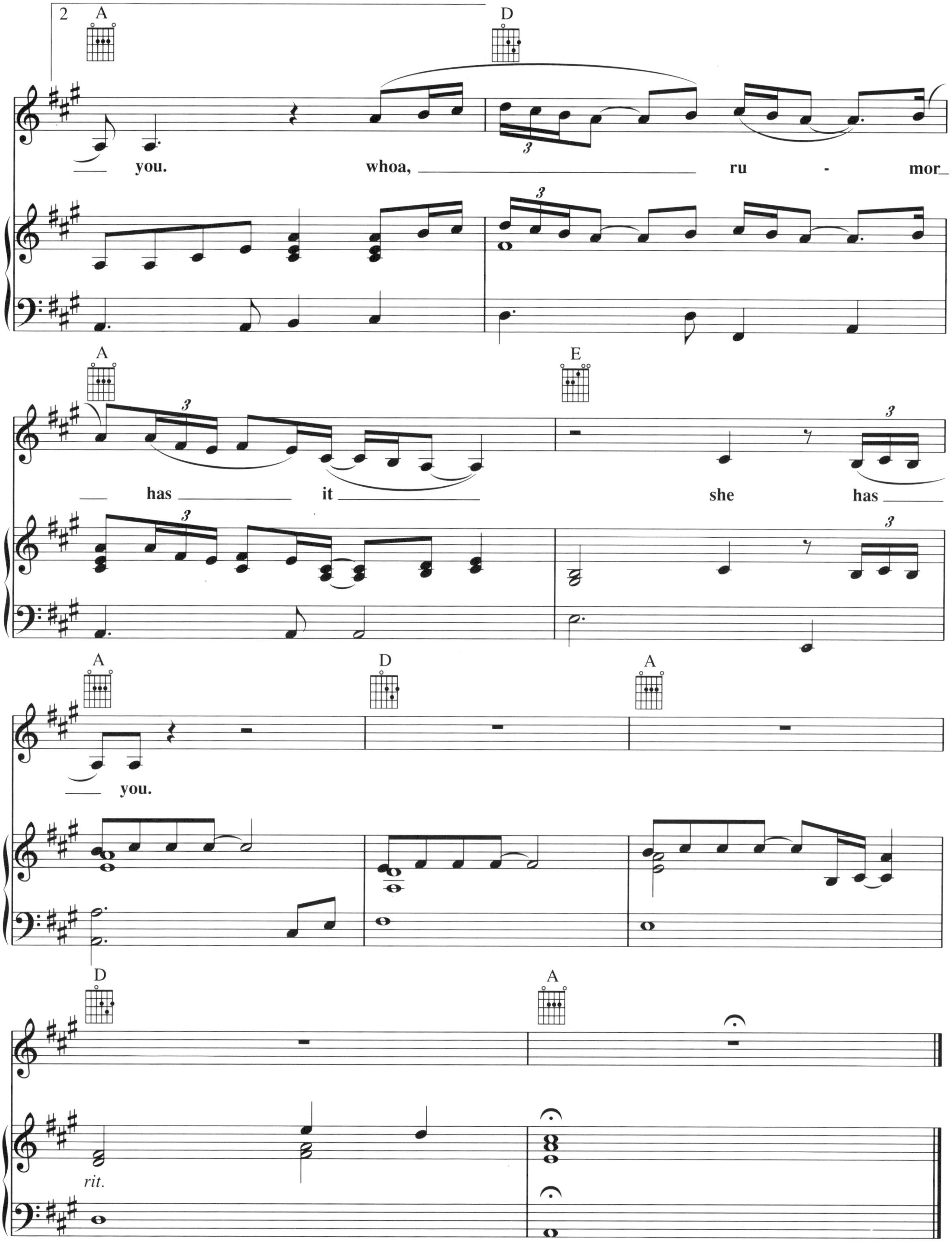
2
A
D
you.
whoa,
ru - mor
A
E
has
it
she
has
A
D
A
you.
D
A
rit.

RESTLESS

Words and Music
by CARL PERKINS

Fast Country Two-beat

walked up to a win-dow. I said, "Give me a tick-et please."
hon-ey, tell___ that driv-er, put his big___ foot___ on the

Instrumental solo

Copyright © 1969 Cedarwood Publishing
International Copyright Secured   All Rights Reserved

She said, "Where to Mis - ter?" I said,
gas and run this old grey dog just as
F7
"That's all right with me 'cause I'm rest - less."
long as it might last. I'm
rest - less.
I need to get out of this
C
town.
Go right now.

Take me where the livin's easy.

Baby that's where I'll be found.

(1st time:) **Well,**

Instrumental solo ends **I said,**

"Honey, tell that driver, take me further down the road.
Just take this old grey dog any place she wants to go." I'm restless.
I need to get on out

I'm trav-'lin' light 'cause I might be goin' far.
I'm takin' nothin' but my old red guitar 'cause I'm restless.

of town.

Take me where the livin's eas - y.

Ba - by, that's where I'll be found.

Solo ends

be found.

Take me where the livin's eas-y.

Ba-by, that's where I'll be found.

D.S. and Fade
(Instrumental ad lib.)

SHAMELESS

Moderately

Words and Music by
BILLY JOEL

Well, I'm shame-less when it comes to
shame-less Ba - by I don't

lov - ing you.___ I'd do an - y-thing you want me to. I'd do an - y-thing at
have a prayer.___ An - y - time I see you stand-ing there I go down up - on my

© 1988 JOEL SONGS
All Rights Controlled and Administered by EMI BLACKWOOD MUSIC INC.
All Rights Reserved   International Copyright Secured   Used by Permission

C	B♭/C		G	

all.____ And I'm stand-ing here for all the
knees.____ And I'm chang-ing. I swore I'd nev-er

D/F#		Em	

world to see.____ ah There ain't that much left of me that has ver-y far
com-pro-mise.____ ah But you con-vinced me oth-er-wise. I'll do an-y-thing

C	B♭/C	D	B/D#

to fall.____ You know__ I'm not a man who's ev-er been in-se-
you please.____ You see in all my__ life I've nev-er found what I

Em		Am7	

cure a-bout the world__ I've been__ liv-ing in.____ I
could-n't re - sist, what I could-n't turn down. I could

Lyrics:

don't break eas - y. I have my pride. But if you need to be sat - is - fied I'm
walk a - way from an - y - one I ev - er knew but I
can't walk a - way from you. I have
nev - er let an - y - thing have this much con - trol o - ver me. I
worked too hard to call my life my own. Well, I

made my-self a world _ and it worked so _ per-fect-ly. _ But it's your world now. I can't re-fuse. _ I nev-er had so much to lose. _ I'm shame-less.

You know it should be eas-y for a man who's strong to say he's sor-ry or ad-mit where he's wrong. I've nev-er lost an-y-thing I ev-er missed, but I've nev-er been in love like this. It's out of my hands. I'm

G
D/F#
shame - less. _ I don't have the pow - er now. ____ But I don't want it
shame - less. _ (vocal ad lib.)
Em
C
B♭/C
an - y - how. _ So I've got to let it go. ____ I'm
G
D/F#
shame - less, _ shame-less as a man can be. _ You can make a to - tal
Em
C
B♭/C
Repeat and Fade
fool of me. _ I just want-ed you to know. ____ I'm

SHE AND I

Words and Music
by DAVE LOGGINS

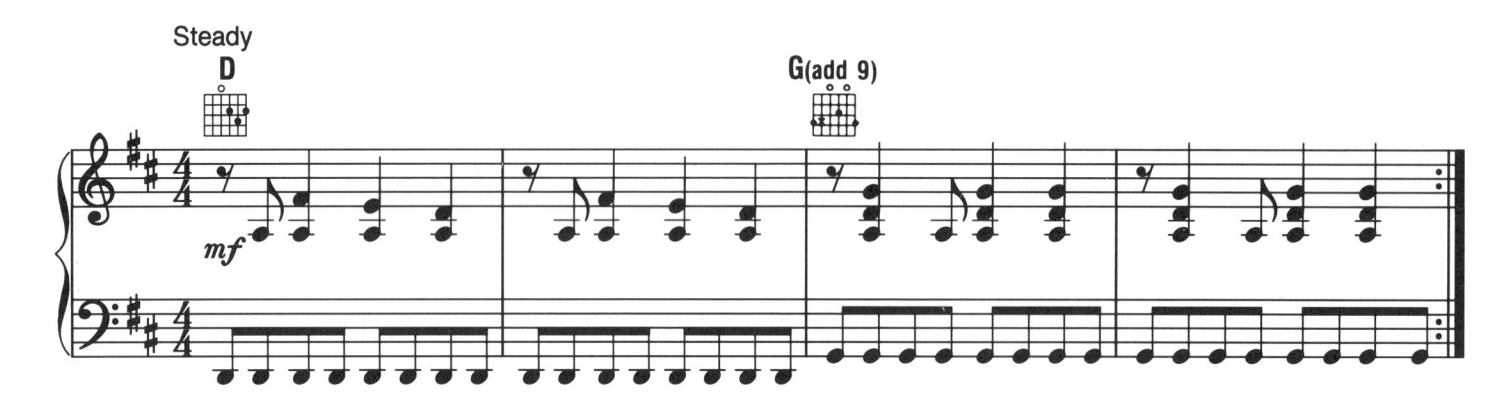

She and I live in our own little world,
She and I share with ev-'ry-bod-y else don't

wor-ry 'bout the world out-side.
same wants, needs and de-si-res.

She and I a-gree
She and I save

© Copyright 1986 by MCA MUSIC PUBLISHING, A Division of MCA INC., and PATCHWORK MUSIC, 1755 Broadway, New York, NY 10019
International Copyright Secured   All Rights Reserved
MCA music publishing

she and I lead a per-fect-ly nor-mal life.
she and I pay on ev-'ry-thing we ac-quire.

Ah, but just be-cause we aren't of-ten seen so-cial-ly,
Ah, but just be-cause we aren't of-ten seen sep-'rate-ly,

peo-ple think we've some-thing to hide. But all our friends know we're
peo-ple think we live one life. It's hard for them to see how

just a lit-tle old fash-ioned, she and I.
an-y-one could be as close as she and I. Oh, ain't it

great (ain't it great), ain't it fine (ain't it fine) to have a love (a love), some-one (some-one) that oth-ers can't find? Ain't it won-der-ful to know all we ev-er need is just the two of us, she and I. So won-der-ful, she and I. Ah,

229

Someday

By ALAN JACKSON
and JIM McBRIDE

Freely, no chord

She looked me in the eye and said, "It's o-ver.

Moderately slow

I can't take this heart-ache an-y-more." She said,

"Don't tell me lies and try to please me. I've

Copyright © 1991 SEVENTH SON MUSIC, MATTIE RUTH MUSICK and EMI APRIL MUSIC INC.
International Copyright Secured   All Rights Reserved

heard it all so many times before." And I took her by the arms and said, "Don't leave me. There's nothing in this world I wouldn't do. Just give me time, I'll be the man you've needed." She said, "I

G
C
Dm
C7/E
wish that I could take that for the truth." And I said,
F
C/E
Dm
"Some-day I'll get my
C
life straight." And she said, "It's
G
G7
too late, what's done is

C
Dm
C7/E
done."
And I told her,
8
F
C/E
Dm
"Some - day."
She said, "I
C
Am
can't wait,
'cause some - times
G
F
G
To Coda
some - day
just nev - er

comes." She said, "All I've ever wanted was to love you, and somewhere deep inside me I still do. And now I think it's time I stopped believing, 'cause I'm nev-er gon-na see a change in you. And I said,

CODA

comes. Oh, some-times

some-day just nev-er

comes."

rit.

SOMEWHERE IN MY BROKEN HEART

Words and Music by BILLY DEAN
and RICHARD LEIGH

You made up your mind it was
I would not have chosen the

time it was o - ver after we had come so far.
road you have tak - en. It has left us miles a - part.

But I think there's e - nough piec - es
But I think I can still find the

© Copyright 1989 EMI BLACKWOOD MUSIC INC. (BMI), EMI APRIL MUSIC INC. and LION-HEARTED MUSIC
All Rights for LION-HEARTED MUSIC Controlled and Administered by EMI APRIL MUSIC INC.
All Rights Reserved International Copyright Secured Used by Permission

Fmaj7
Esus
E7
F
C/G
G
of for - give - ness some-where in my bro - ken heart.
will to keep go - ing some-where in my bro - ken heart.
1 C
2 C
F
So fly.
D.S., Instrumental solo
G/F
F
C
G6
F6/G
Go a - head and fly un - til you find out who you are.
C
F
And I, I will
Instrumental solo ends

keep my love un-spo-ken, some-where in my bro-ken heart. I hope that in time you will find what you long for. Love that's writ-ten in the stars. And when you fin-'lly do, I think

2nd time: rit.   *a tempo*

To Coda
Fmaj7
Esus
E7
F
C/G
G
you will see it's some-where in my bro - ken heart.
C
D.S. al Coda
CODA
F
C/G
G7
some-where in my bro - ken,
F
F/G
G
F
C/G
G
some-where in my bro - ken, some-where in my bro - ken,
rit.
C
C/E
Fmaj7
C/G
G7
C
heart.
a tempo
rit.

STRONG ENOUGH TO BEND

Words and Music by DON SCHLITZ
and BETH NIELSON CHAPMAN

Bright two-beat

1. There's a tree out in the back-yard that nev-er has been
2. years we have stayed in to-geth-er
3,4. tree out in the back-yard that nev-er has been

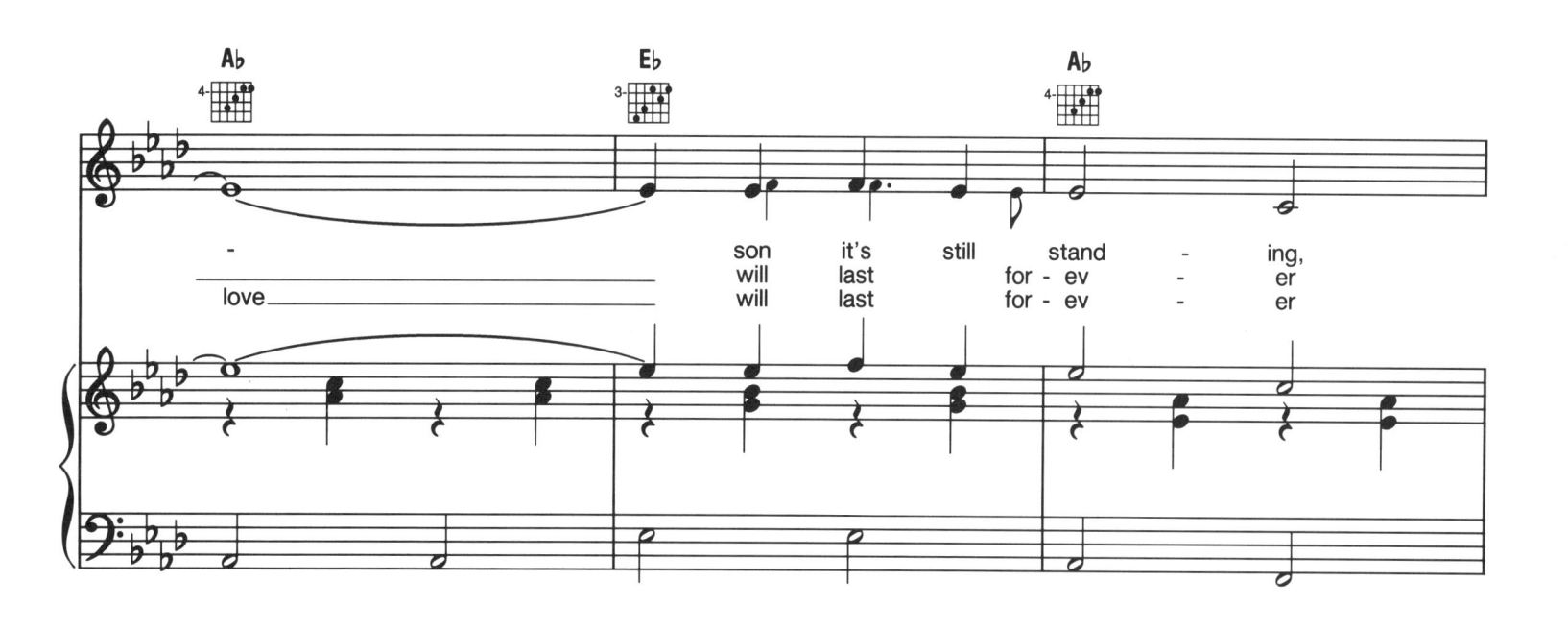

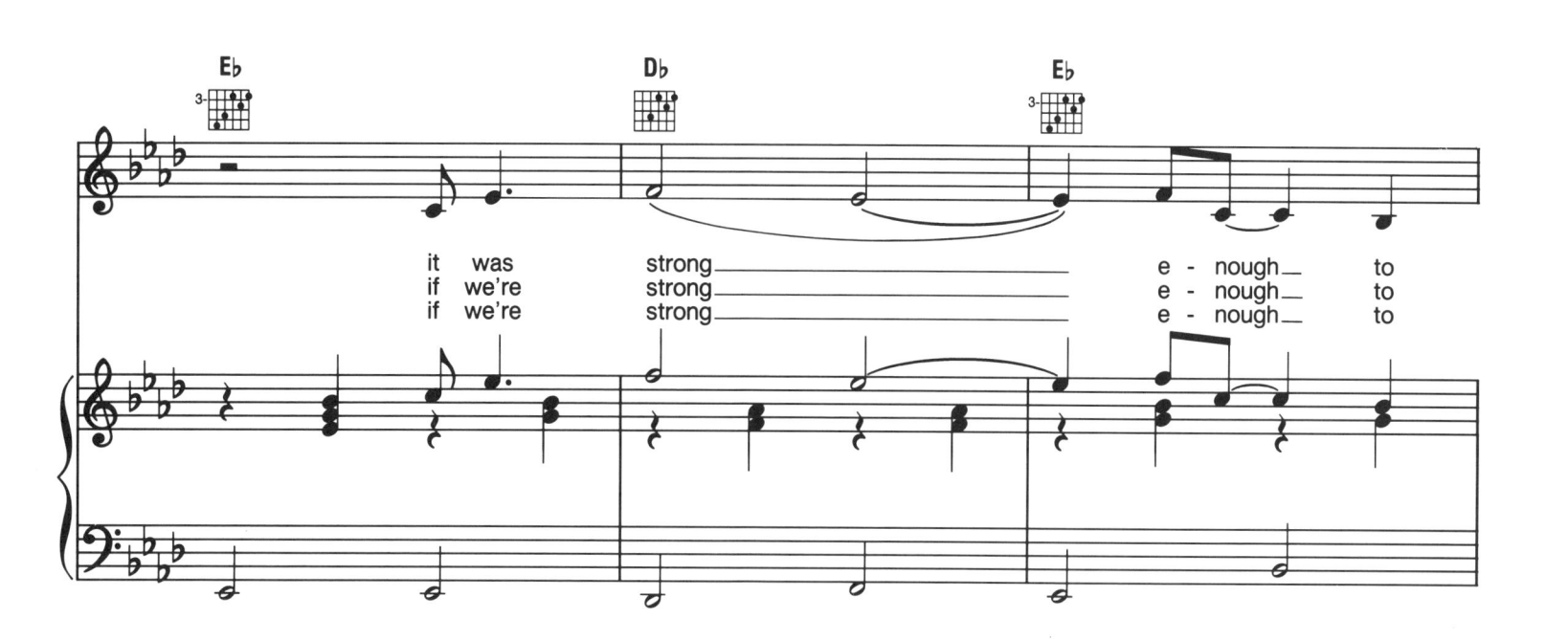

bro - ken by the wind.
and as friends.
bro - ken by the wind, And the rea-
What our we have

- love
son it's still stand - ing, will last for - ev - er
will last for - ev - er

it was strong e - nough to
if we're strong e - nough to
if we're strong e - nough to

A♭
To Coda
1
2,3
bend.
bend.
bend.
For
When
When
B♭7
you say some-thing that you can't take back,
you start think-ing that you know it all,
D♭
a big wind blows and you hear a lit-tle crack.
a big wind blows and a branch will fall.
B♭7
When you say hey, well I
When you say hey, this

might be wrong,
job takes two,
you can
we can
Eb
Db
1
Cm
(Sway with the wind till the
sway with the wind till the storm is gone.
sway with the wind till the skies turn blue.
Bbm
storm is gone.)
2
Cm
Bbm
(Sway with the wind till the skies turn blue.)
D.S. al Coda
Like a tree
Like the tree

CODA
E♭
Our love will last for -
A♭
E♭
D♭
ev - er if we're strong
E♭
A♭
E♭
A♭
e - nough to bend.

A Sunday Kind of Love

Words and Music by BARBARA BELLE, LOUIS PRIMA,
ANITA LEONARD and STAN RHODES

I _____ want a Sun-day kind_ of love,
a love _ to last _ past _ Sat-ur-day night. _
And I'd _ like to know _____ it's more than love _ of first sight.

© Copyright 1946, 1972 by MCA MUSIC PUBLISHING, A Division of MCA INC.,
1755 Broadway, New York, NY 10019
Copyright Renewed
International Copyright Secured   All Rights Reserved
MCA music publishing

246

247

G
no chord
Ab7
G7
C
C#dim7
way. And my arms need some-one to in-put
Dm7
G7
C
C7
to keep me warm when Mon-days and Tues-days
F
Fm
C
A7
grow cold. And I need a love for all my life to have and to hold.
D9
G7
1 C
Bb9
C
no chord
G7#5
D.S.
I need a Sun-day kind of love.

2 C
B♭7
A7
Dm7
love, oh yeah. On a Mon-day or a Tues-day
B♭9
Em7
a Wed-n'sday or a Thurs-day, Fri-day or
A9
Dm7
Sat-ur-day. I don't want noth-in' ba-by,
G7
no chord
C
A♭
G7
Cmaj9
I want a Sun-day kind of love.
rit.

TEMPTED

Words and Music by MARTY STUART
and PAUL KENNERLEY

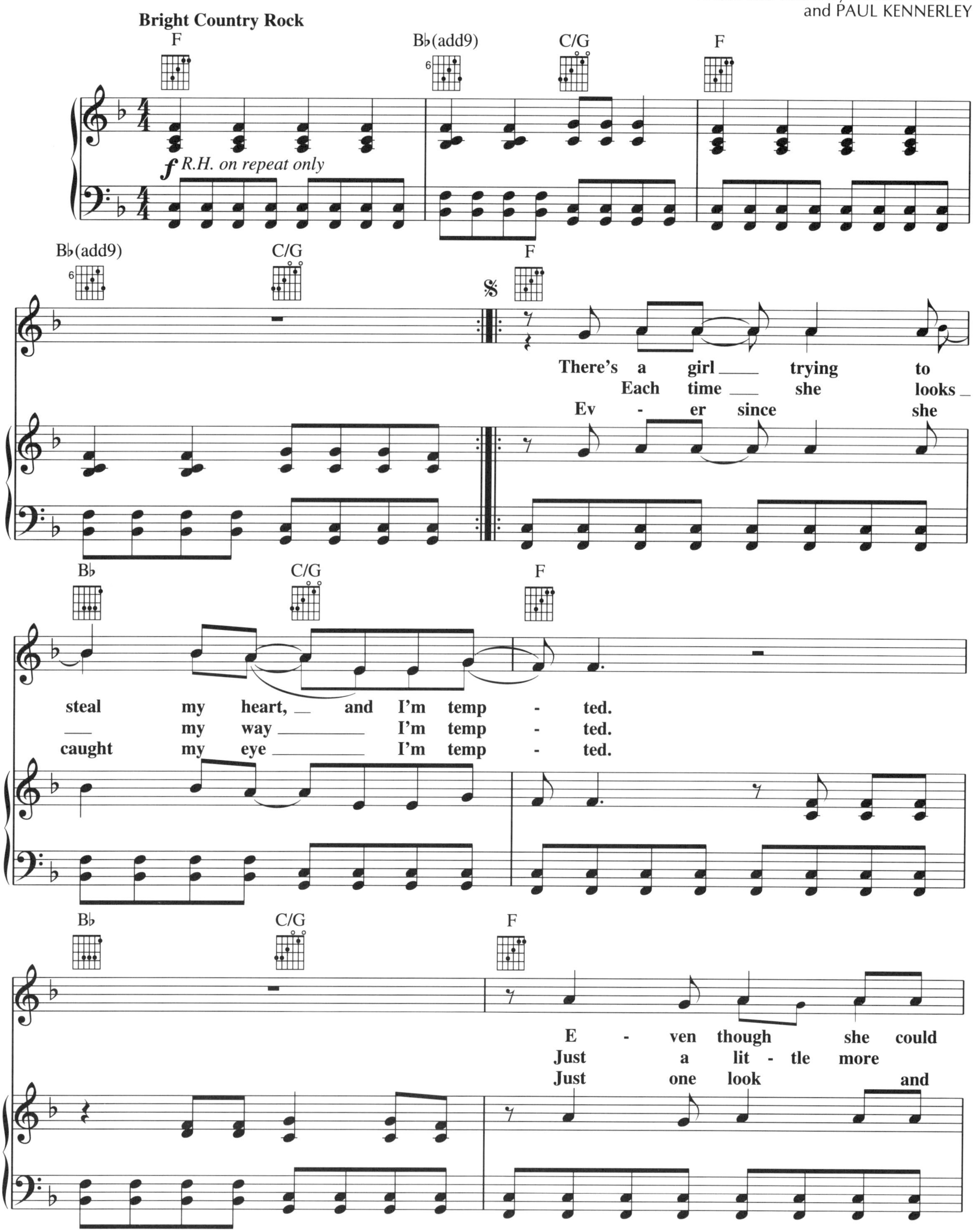

tear it a - part, I'm temp - ted.
ev - 'ry day ___ I'm temp - ted.
you'll know ___ why ___ I'm temp - ted.

In her eyes there's mys - ter - y.
It's so hard to re - sist
So, if I'm burned by the flame

Ev - 'ry time she smiles at ___ me
the thought ___ of her ___ sweet ___ kiss.
there's no one but me to ___ blame

I know ___ how it ___ could be, ___ and I'm temp -
Can't take much more of this. ___ I'm temp -
'cause ev - 'ry time she calls ___ my name ___ I'm temp -

F
B♭
C
1 F
- ted.
- ted.
- ted.
B♭
C
2,3
F
C
Temp - ted and tried.
F7
B♭
F
Deep down in - side I can't de -
C
F
B♭
C
To Coda
ny that I'm temp - ted.

Tempt - ed___ and tried.

Deep down _____ inside _____ I can't _____ deny that I'm tempted. I'm tempted. I'm tempted. I'm tempted.

cresc.

(SMOOTH AS) TENNESSEE WHISKEY

255

Words and Music by DEAN DILLON
and LINDA HARGROVE

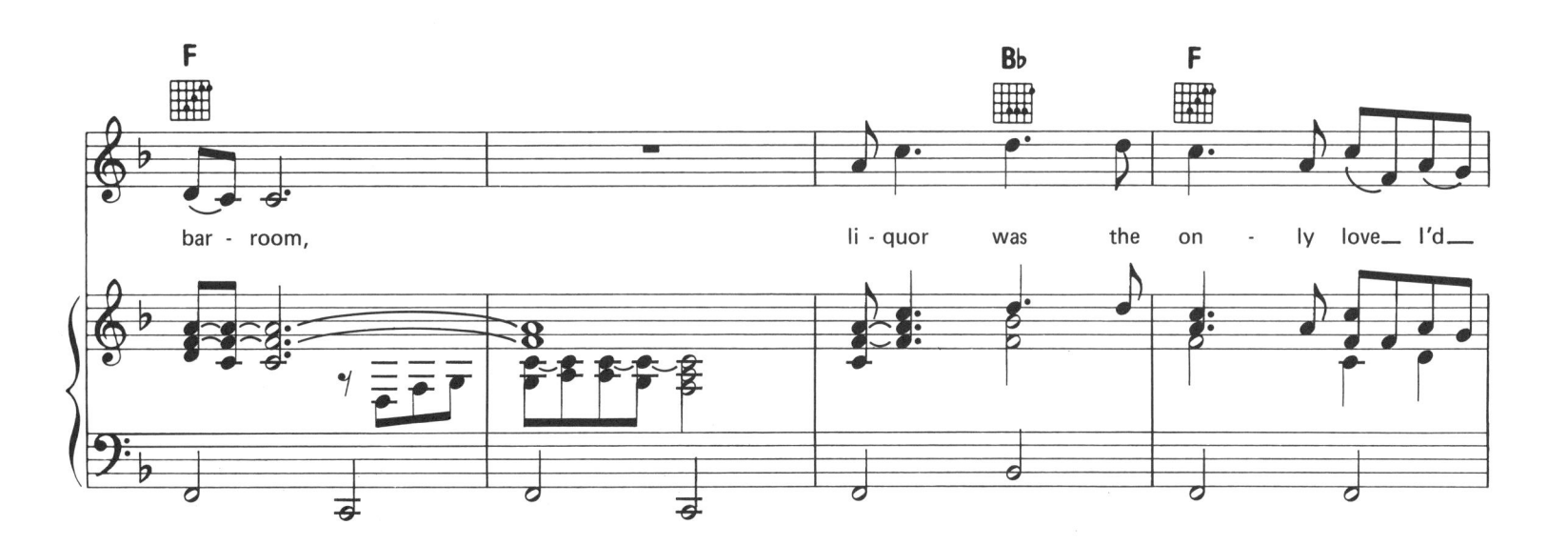

I used to spend my nights out in a bar-room, li-quor was the on-ly love I'd known. But you res-cued me from reach-in' for the

Copyright © 1981, 1983 Songs of PolyGram International, Inc. and Algee Music Corporation
International Copyright Secured   All Rights Reserved

bot - tom,__ and you brought me back from be - ing__ too far__ gone. You're as__ smooth_____ as Tenn-es-see whis - key.____ You're as sweet_____ __ as straw-ber-ry wine. You're as__ warm_____ as a glass of bran-dy, and I stay stoned on your love all the time.

I looked for love in all the same old pla-ces, found the bot-tom of the

G D G
bot-tle al - ways dry. But when you poured out your
C G
heart I did - n't waste it, 'cause there's
C G/D D7 G C D
noth-ing like your love to get me high. You're as
G C G
smooth as Tenn-es - see whis - key. You're as

sweet _____ as straw-ber-ry - wine. You're as _____ warm _____ as a glass _ of bran-dy, and I stay stoned on your love all __ the time. I stay stoned on your love all __ the time.

THANKS AGAIN

Gently flowing

Words and Music by
JIM RUSHING

I've sent bouquets_ for Mother's Day, for Father's Day a shirt and a card._ And while they came from the heart,_ they all_ fell short of saying how special you both_ are._ It

© Copyright 1987, 1988 by PolyGram International Publishing, Inc. and Amanda-Lin Music
International Copyright Secured   All Rights Reserved

A
E/A
was - n't till I was up and gone,
young man, least I think I am, but I'm
D/A
A
mar - ried with a cou - ple of kids of my own,
watch - in' my own hair turn gray. And your
C#7sus
C#7
F#m
Esus
D
do - ing what ma - mas and dad - dies do that I
call last Sun - day brought to mind that I
Bm
E
Esus
E
re - al - ized what I must have put you through.
owe you a debt I can nev - er re - pay.

262

So thanks a-gain____ for the love in the cra-dle and
So thanks a-gain____ for wor-ryin' and wait-in' and when

all of the chang-es____ that kept me dry. And
I start-ed dat-in' on week-end nights. And

thanks a-gain____ for the love at our ta-ble and
thanks a-gain____ for the help with my home-work and

tan-nin' my bot-tom when I told you a lie,____ for
sit-tin' up with____ me till I got it right,____ for your

tak-ing me fish-in' and fly-in' my kites, and tuck-in' me in yes night
car for the prom, your let-ters in Nam, but most of all, Dad-dy, for

af-ter night. To my beau-ti-ful life-long friends, hey,
mar-ry-in' mom.

Mom and Dad-dy, thanks a-gain.

I'm still a Mom and Dad-dy, thanks again. To my beau-ti-ful life-long friends, hey, Mom and Dad-dy, thanks a-gain.

Spoken: Thanks again.

THERE FOR A WHILE

Words and Music by ANNA LISA GRAHAM
and CURTIS WRIGHT

Country ballad

For so long I was lookin' for a reason to make livin' worth while
guess I never asked you, a-fraid of what the an-swer might be.

I

I found that rea - son when I first saw you
you love me for - ev - er, nev - er want - ing to be free?
G
smile.
There was no
I
C
F
ques - tion you were the an - swer for a part - ner with no dan - cer or no
had no way of know - in' just how soon you'd be go - in' a -
C
song.
way.
You
Would

set my life to mu - sic _____ the day ___ you came __ a -
it have made a ___ dif - f'rence _____ if on - ly I _____ asked __ you to

long.
stay. And there for a while ___
Now, I don't know ___ what

all of my dreams __ come __ true. _____
my life could hold ___ for __ me _____ 'cause

There for a while _____ there was noth - in' _____
I know that I _____ had it all _____ when you __ were

G7sus
G7
I couldn't do.
hold - in' me.
Yes,
F
G
there for a while the fu - ture was fin - 'ly clear
C
E
F
'cause there for a while,
G
1 C
E
there for a while you were here.

F
G
C
Fmaj9
G
2 Am
C/G
F♯m7♭5
F
C/E
I here. Yes,
Dm7
G
there for a while, there for a while you were
F
C/E
Dm7
Csus
C
here.
rit.

THERE'S A TEAR IN MY BEER

Words and Music by
HANK WILLIAMS

Plaintively

There's A Tear In My Beer 'cause I'm cryin' for you, Dear
night I walked the floor and the night be- fore
You are on my lonely mind In-
You are on my lonely mind It
to these last nine beers I have shed a million tears You are
seems my life is through And I'm so dog-gone blue You are
on my lonely mind I'm gonna keep on
on my lonely mind I'm gonna keep on

Copyright © 1952 by Acuff-Rose-Opryland Music, Inc.
Copyright Renewed, Assigned to Acuff-Rose-Opryland Music, Inc. and Aberbach Enterprises, Ltd. (Rightsong Music, Administrator) for the U.S.A. only.
All rights outside the U.S.A. controlled by Acuff-Rose-Opryland Music, Inc.
International Copyright Secured   All Rights Reserved

271

These Lips Don't Know How to Say Goodbye

Words and Music by
HARLAN HOWARD

Country ballad

Once I promised I'd do any-thing to please you,
ask me for the stars that shine a-bove you,
and looking back you must admit I've tried.
then I could come much closer to the mark.

Copyright © 1972 by Tree Publishing Co., Inc.
All Rights Administered by Sony Music Publishing, 8 Music Square West, Nashville, TN 37203
International Copyright Secured   All Rights Reserved

Now you stand there___ and tell me I must___
So don't stand___ there and tell me not to___

leave you, but I can't___ go.___
love you un - less you stop the

Well, I guess I must have___ lied.___
beat - ing of my___ heart.___

For these lips___ don't know how___ to say good -

274

1 C
- bye.
If you'd
2 C
bye
No, these
G7
lips don't know how to say good - bye.
C
rit.

THINGS ARE TOUGH ALL OVER

Words and Music by LISA SILVER
and TREY BRUCE

MCA music publishing

I can't imagine what you want with me.
So if you're calling me for sympathy

You must have come up short tonight. I thought
'cause I'm getting harder to forget, I won't be

you were happy being free, but your voice tells me that's not right.
a one night remedy to help you live with your

regret. Guess things are tough all

o - ver, e - ven on the sin - gle side of town. Guess it's hard - er than you thought it'd be with - out my lov - ing arms a - round. And now the beat - ing of your lone - ly__ heart _____ is the cold___ night's on - ly sound.__

Guess things are tough__ all__

o - ver when old mem - 'ries__ get _____

you __ down.

2 G
C
when old mem - 'ries get you down.
Fmaj7
F6
Guess things are tough all o - ver
G
F
when old mem - 'ries get you down.
C/E
Dm
C
rit.

TURN IT LOOSE

Words and Music by DON SCHLITZ,
BRENT MAHER and CRAIG BICKHARDT

Lively Blues feel

Some call it coun-try with a
feel like danc-ing and you

lit-tle bit of rhy-thm and blues.
just can't stay in your seat.

© Copyright 1987 by MCA MUSIC PUBLISHING, A Division of MCA INC., DON SCHLITZ MUSIC, WELBECK MUSIC, BLUE QUILL MUSIC and COLGEMS-EMI MUSIC, INC.
Rights of DON SCHLITZ MUSIC, WELBECK MUSIC and BLUE QUILL MUSIC administered by MCA MUSIC PUBLISHING, A Division of MCA INC., 1755 Broadway, New York, NY 10019
International Copyright Secured   All Rights Reserved
MCA music publishing

And when the boys start rock-ing, there's a
Your knees start knock-ing and you

beat that you just can't lose.
can't help stomp-ing your feet.

Where it's gon-na take us, no-
Be-fore you ev-en know it, you'll be

-bod-y knows; it sure feels good to the bod-y and
sing-ing a-long; it makes me want to stay here all night

Em
G
F
C/E
soul.
long.
I love the slide of a
G
F/G
C/G
G
F
C/E
steel guitar, I love the moan of an
G
F/G
C/G
Em
F
C
old blues harp.
I love the
G
F
C/E
G
F/G
C/G
shake of a tam - bou - rine, I love the

bass _____ when it's low and mean. _____ So put on your shout-in' shoes, _____ and turn it loose, _____ and turn it loose. _____ You _____ turn it loose. _____

F
C6
Gsus2
Uh!
F
C6
Mm,
loose!
D(no3rd)
D.S. al Coda
I love the
CODA
G
F/G
C/G
G
F/G
C/G
G
F/G
C/G
F
C
Repeat and Fade
and turn it loose,

This One's Gonna Hurt You
(For A Long, Long Time)

Words and Music by
MARTY STUART

Moderate country swing (♪♪ played as ♩♪)

Ba - by, close that suit - case, let's turn this thing a - round. We've got
bot - tle on the ta - ble to help me un - der - stand how a

ev - 'ry - bod - y talk - in' be - tween a
love can go so wrong

Copyright © 1992 Songs Of PolyGram International, Inc. and Tubb's Bus Music
International Copyright Secured All Rights Reserved

287

long, long _____ time. There's a
long, long _____
time. A long, _____ long _____
time _____ is _____ for - ev - er. _____ And _ will
I _____ get _ o - ver you, _____ prob - 'bly nev -

er. You can't walk away from true love and leave your feelings all behind. 'Cause this one's gonna hurt you for a long, long time.

You __ can't __ walk a - way from

true love and leave your feel-ings all be-hind. Ah, this one's gonna hurt you for a long, long time.

'Til A Tear Becomes A Rose

Words and Music by BILL RICE
and MARY SHARON RICE

grows. But if you weep I'll be right here to hold you 'til each tear you cry becomes a rose.

(Female:) Dear-est

love, _____ I know your heart _____ is shat-tered _____ and all ___ my ___ words _____ can of-fer no re-lief. _____

night _____ when mem-'ries tend _____ to gath-er _____ lay ___ with ___ me _____ and put your fears to sleep. _____

But my _____
'Cause there's no _____

love ____ will heal the pain ____ you've
pain ____ no dream can put ____ a-

suf - fered ____ and I'll be ____
sun - der, ____ all ____ the ____

here ____ if you should turn to
love that binds us, you and

me. ____
me. ____

(Both:) Dar - ling, I can

see__ the clouds a - round__ you and in your__ heart I know a sor - row grows. But if you weep I'll be__ right here__ to hold__ you

Cm
F
'til each tear you cry becomes a
1
B♭
rose.
(Male:) In deep - est
2
B♭
F/A
Gm
F
rose.
'Til each tear you
B♭
F
B♭
cry becomes a rose.
3
3
3
3

Turn It On, Turn It Up, Turn Me Loose

Words and Music by KOSTAS
and WAYLAND PATTON

With a steady beat

Well, I'm back again for another night
tear should fall if I should whisper her name

Copyright © 1990 by Songs Of PolyGram International, Inc., PolyGram International Publishing, Inc. and Amanda-Lin Music
International Copyright Secured   All Rights Reserved

299

300

E
mem - 'ry, it's driv - ing me lone - ly,
A
cra - zy and blue. It helps me for -
get her, so the loud - er, the bet - ter. Hey,
E
B
To Coda
Mis - ter turn it on, turn it up, turn me loose.

Lyrics:
Now, if a
Turn it on loose.
Yeah, Mister, turn it on turn it up, turn me loose.

WHEN YOU SAY NOTHING AT ALL

Words and Music by DON SCHLITZ
and PAUL OVERSTREET

you can light up the dark.
you drown out the crowd.

Try as I may ___ I could nev - er ex - plain ___
Old Mis - ter Web - ster could nev - er de - fine ___

what I hear ___ when you don't ___ say a thing. ___
what's be - ing said ___ be - tween your ___ heart and mine. ___ } The

smile on your face ___ lets me know ___ that you need ___ me. There's a

truth in your eyes ___ say-ing you'll ___ nev-er leave ___ me. A

touch of your hand ___ says you'll catch ___ me if ev - er I fall. ___

Now you say it best ___ when you say noth-ing at all. ___

when you say noth-ing at all. ___

The

when you say noth-ing at all.

THE WHISKEY AIN'T WORKIN'

Words and Music by RONNY SCAIFE
and MARTY STUART

Easy Country Two-beat

There was a time I could drink my cares away and drawn out all of the heart-aches that hurt me night and day.

Copyright © 1990 Songs Of PolyGram International, Inc. and Partner Music
International Copyright Secured   All Rights Reserved

When the thought of you came crashin' through, I'd have one more. But now, the whis-key ain't work-in' an-y-more. I need one good honk-y-tonk an-gel to turn my life a-round. That's rea-son e-nough for me to lay this ol' bot-tle down. Well, a wom-an warm and will-in' that's

(2nd verse) an warm and will-in', Lord, that's a-

what I'm look-in' for 'cause the whis-key ain't
what I'm look-in' for 'cause the whis-key ain't

work-in' an-y-more.
work-in' an-y-

They knew my name at ev-ery bar in town and they knew all of the rea-sons why I was com-in' 'round, 'round, 'round.

(Spoken:) Sing it Travis. *(Sung:)* 'Cause in my mind, peace I'd find

when they'd start to pour. But now, the whis-key ain't work-in' an-y-more. I, I need more. Lord, the whis-key ain't work-in' an-y-more. *(Spoken:) That's for sure!*

WHOLE LOTTA HOLES

Words and Music by DON HENRY
and JON VEZNER

Moderate Country Shuffle

Hey look, ___ there's a hole ___ in my floor-
___ in the toes ___ of my stock-
be a hole ___ in my ceil-

-board. ___ What's that, ___ there's a hole ___ in my jeans. ___ And who ___
-ings, ___ and there's gold ___ in the holes ___ in my teeth. ___ And who ___
-ing, ___ 'cause this rain ___ keeps fall-ing on me. ___ I'm be-

Copyright © 1989 Cross Keys Publishing Co., Inc. and Sheddhouse Music
All Rights for Cross Keys Publishing Co., Inc. administered by Sony Music Publishing, 8 Music Square West, Nashville, TN 37203
All Rights for Sheddhouse Music managed worldwide by PolyGram International Publishing, Inc.
International Copyright Secured   All Rights Reserved

Bm G A G
left that hole in my clos - et? Well there's a hole in my bed where
left that hole in my wal - let, and a hole in my chest where my heart
gin-ning to feel this feel - ing like there's a hole in my head for
A Bm G D
he used to be.
used to be?
let - tin' him leave.
I got a whole lot - ta holes in my life. I got a whole
Bm G D Bm G
lot - ta holes in my life. If you stacked 'em all to - geth - er, you could

fall in there for - ev - er. Got a whole __ lot - ta holes in my __ life. __

Well, there's holes __

A Asus2 A Bm D A
D.S. al Coda
Well, there must
CODA
Bm G A
I got a whole lot - ta holes in my life,
Bm G A Bm D
my life. Got a whole lot - ta holes in my life.
A Asus2 Bm D A Asus2
Repeat and Fade

THE WOMAN BEFORE ME

Words and Music by
JUDE JOHNSTONE

Moderately slow

I ___ can see you

turn a-way.   When I ask what   for, ___ you say ___ it is-n't
ar-gu-ment   it will show, ___ when you ___ go a lit-tle
nev-er be   like the past, ___ what-ev-er kind of

an-y-thing.   But I'm not   sure. ___ Some-thin' un-der-
far-ther than   you meant to   go. ___ I ___ know you don't
mem-o-ries   that you   have. ___ Noth-in's gon-na

Copyright © 1991 Mad Jack Music (BMI)
Administered by Bug Music, Inc.
International Copyright Secured   All Rights Reserved

neath the skin___ won't let you__ be.___ And_ you try to keep it in__
mean the things_ that you__ say.__ I__ just wan-na ease the pain_
hurt you now.__ Can't you__ see? I__ al-read-y made a vow_

but I can see.__ The wom-an be-fore__ me must have been hard on you__ 'cause that
that's in your way.__ But the
that I can keep.__ But the

hurt in your eyes, _____ I nev-er put you through. __

Some-times I think _ you must be talk-in' to _ the wom-an be-fore _ me _ and you. _

1. Some - times in an

2.

If there are sor - rows that bring _ back a tear, _

don't let them keep _ us a - part. _

321

You ought to know — you've got noth - ing to fear here in my heart. 'Cause you and I will

Some-times I think — you must be talk-in' to — the wom-an be-fore — me — and you.

YOU AGAIN

Words and Music by
PAUL OVERSTREET and DON SCHLITZ

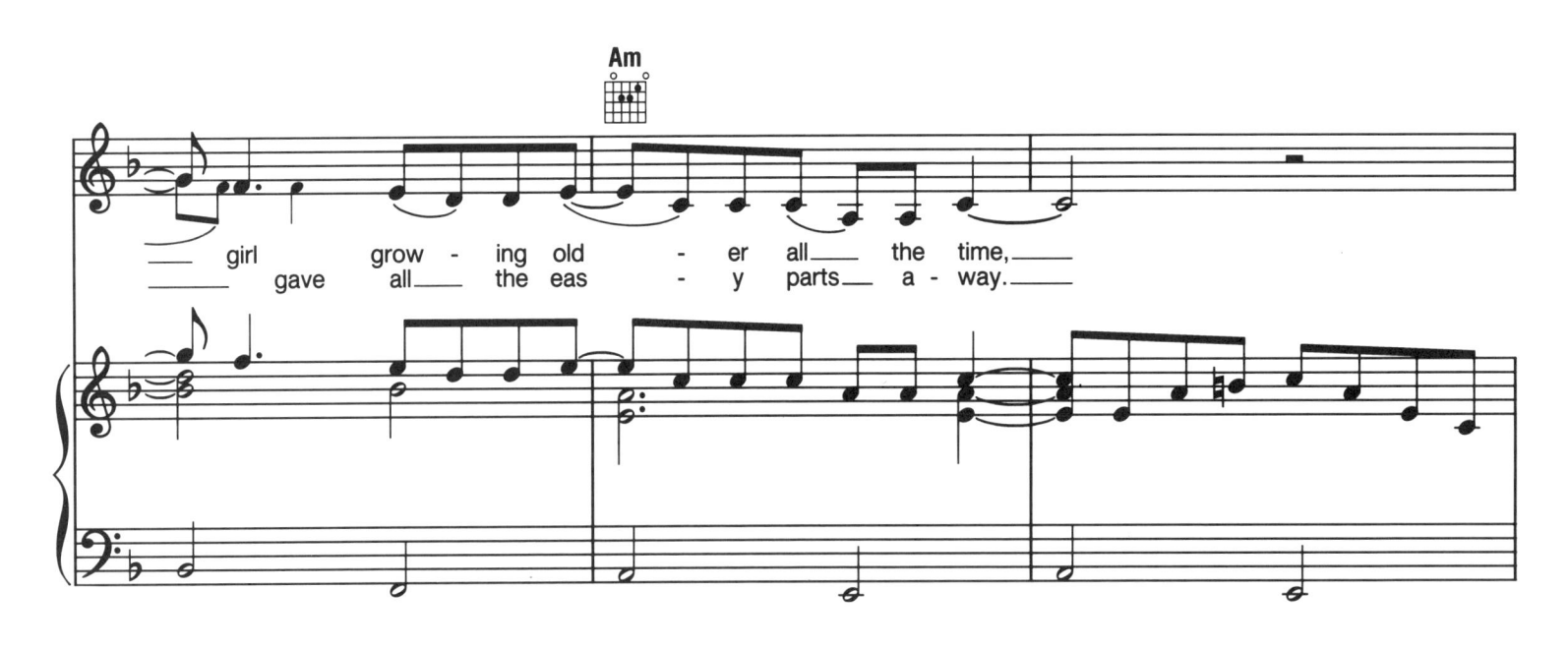

Moderately fast

Looking at my life through the eyes of a young girl growing older all the time,
Times weren't always good, seems like the Lord gave all the easy parts away.

Copyright © 1985 by MCA MUSIC PUBLISHING, A Division of MCA INC., DON SCHLITZ MUSIC and WRITERS GROUP MUSIC
Rights of DON SCHLITZ MUSIC Administered by MCA MUSIC PUBLISHING, A Division of MCA INC., 1755 Broadway, New York, NY 10019
International Copyright Secured   All Rights Reserved

[Sheet music]

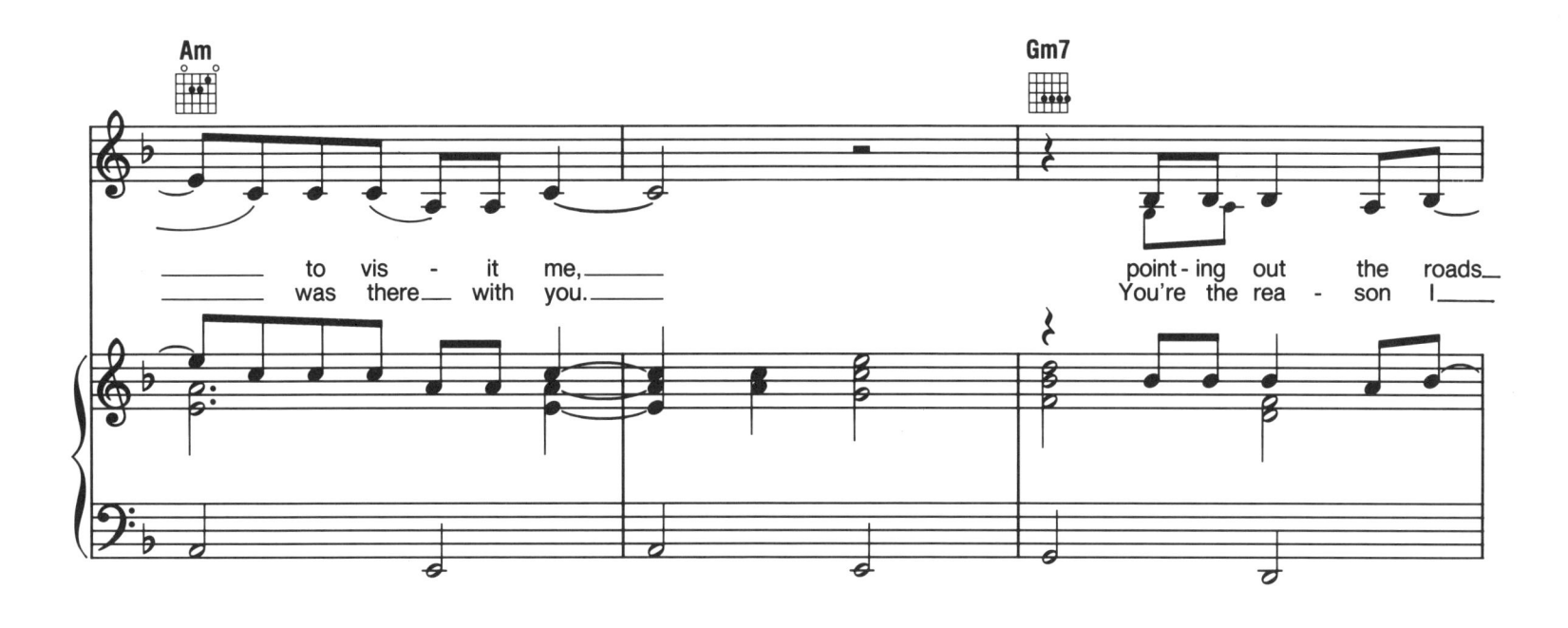

C7
B♭
F/A
not tak - en. So much I'd like to change,
kept go - ing. If I could start my life a - new,
Gm7
C
but one thing I'd do the same
the first thing that I would do
I'd choose
B♭
F
you a - gain, I'd choose you a - gain.
Gm
C
If God gave me the chance to do it all

F
B♭
— a - gain, —
oh, I'd care - ful - ly — con - sid -
F
- er ev - 'ry choice, — and then —
out of all —
(D.S.) I'd lis -
Gm7
C
To Coda
— the boys — in the world —
I'd — choose you —
- ten to — my heart —
and I'd — choose you —
F
1
Gm
C
— a - gain. —

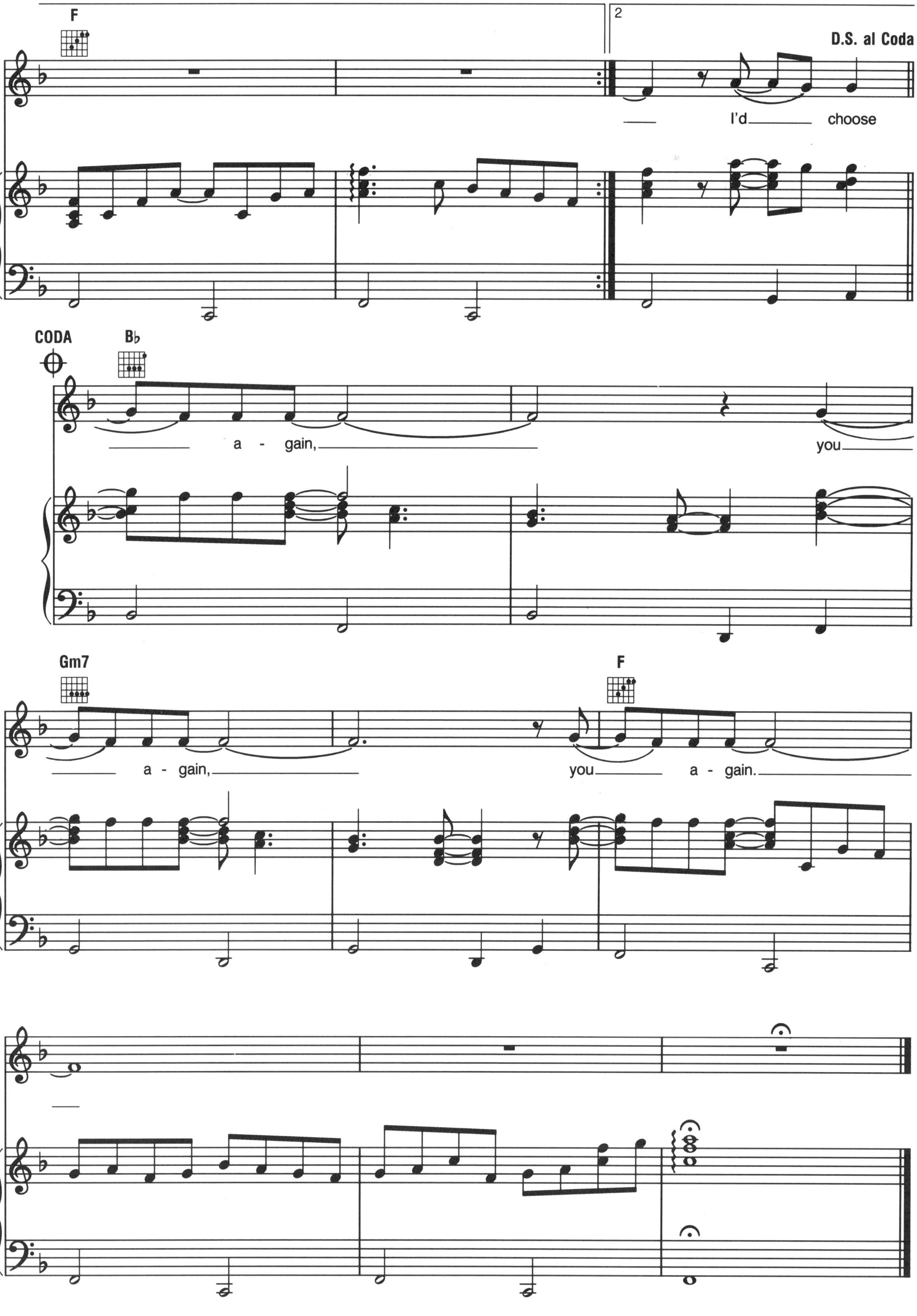
F
2
D.S. al Coda
I'd choose
CODA
B♭
a - gain,
you
Gm7
a - gain,
F
you a - gain.

You Know Me Better Than That

By TONY HASELDEN
and ANNA LISA GRAHAM

Moderate Country

Baby, since you left __ me __ there's some-bod-y new. __
pic-nics and blue __ jeans __ and buck-ets of beer, __ now it's

She thinks I'm per - fect, I swear. __
bal - let and sym - pho - ny hall. __

Copyright © 1990 by Millhouse Music and Sheddhouse Music
All Rights of Millhouse Music Controlled by Songs of PolyGram International, Inc.
All Rights of Sheddhouse Music Controlled by PolyGram International Publishing, Inc.
International Copyright Secured   All Rights Reserved

She likes my bod - y, my class ___ and my charm, ___ she
I'm in - to cul - ture ___ clean ___ up to my ears. ___ It's like

says I've got a con - fi - dent air. ___ She re-
wear - ing a shoe ___ that's ___ too small. ___ Well, I

spects my am - bi - tion. thinks I'm tal - ent - ed too, but she's in
caught her with an is - sue of *Brides* ___ mag - a - zine, ___

love with an im - age time is bound to see ___ through. ___ Oh, ___
star - in' at dress - es ___ and pick - in' out ___ rings. ___ But,

you know me bet - ter than that. ____

You know the me ____ that gets la - zy and fat. ____ How

mood - y I ____ can be, ____ all my in - se - cur - i - ties. ____

You've seen me lose ____ all my charm. ____ You

know I was raised on a farm. Oh, she tells her friends I'm perfect and that I love her cat, but you know me better than that.

B♭
C
F
I miss
2
F
B♭
F/A
Oh, she tells her friends I'm per - fect and that I
Fm/A♭
G7
love that cat,
oh, but you
B♭
C
F
know me bet - ter than that.

You Don't Count The Cost

Words and Music by BUCKY JONES, CHRIS WATERS and TOM SHAPIRO

Easy country ballad

It hap-pens to __ a moth - er __ when she's __ giv-ing birth. Her heart is filled __ with joy __ while her bod-y's filled __ with hurt. She holds the ba - by close __ to her __ de-

hap-pens to __ a sol - dier __ fight-ing for __ his home. Fear wells up in-side __ him __ and yet, he still __ goes __ on __ e-ven though __ he __ knows he may __

hap-pens all __ a-round __ us __ each and ev-'ry-day. Some-one's giv - ing all __ they've __ got __ for some - one else - 's sake. If you ev - er doubt __ it, just

Copyright © 1991 PolyGram International Publishing, Inc., McBEC Music, Edge O' Woods Music, Kinetic Diamond Music, Inc. and Moline Valley Music, Inc.
International Copyright Secured   All Rights Reserved

A
F♯m7
E
spite the pain_ he caused._
be the next_ to fall.___
think a-bout_ the cross.__
When it comes_ to love,______
B7
1
E
you don't count______ the cost.
It
2,3
E
C♯m
A
cost.
You don't count_ the heart-ache. You don't
E
C♯m
A
count the sac - ri-fice._
And all that counts_ is what_ you feel in-

-side. It does-n't real-ly mat-ter what is gained or what is lost. When it comes to love, no, you don't count the cost.

It

CODA
A
E
E/G♯
does-n't real - ly mat-ter what is gained or what is lost
A
E/B
'cause when it comes to love,
B7
E(add9)
you don't count the cost.
A
E
No.
rit.

Your Favorites in COUNTRY MUSIC *and more...*

COUNTRY STANDARDS
A collection of 51 of country's biggest hits including: (Hey Won't You Play) Another Somebody Done Somebody Wrong Song • By The Time I Get To Phoenix • Could I Have This Dance • Daddy Sang Bass • Forever And Ever Amen • Bless The U.S.A. • Green Green Grass Of Home • Islands In The Stream • King Of The Road • Little Green Apples • Lucille • Mammas Don't Let Your Babies Grow Up To Be Cowboys • Ruby Don't Take Your Love To Town • Stand By Me • Through The Years • Your Cheatin' Heart.
00359517 $10.95

COUNTRY MUSIC HALL OF FAME
The Country Music Hall Of Fame Was Founded in 1961 by the Country Music Association (CMA). Each year, new members are elected—and these books are the first to represent all of its members with photos, biography and music selections related to each individual.

Volume 1
Includes: Fred Rose, Hank Williams, Jimmie Rodgers, Roy Acuff, George D. Hay, PeeWee King, Minnie Pearl and Grandpa Jones. 23 songs, including: Blue Eyes Crying In The Rain • Cold, Cold Heart • Wabash Cannon Ball • Tennesse Waltz.
00359510 $8.95

Volume 2
Features: Tex Ritter, Ernest Tubb, Eddy Arnold, Jim Denny, Joseph Lee Frank, Uncle Dave Macon, Jim Reeves and Bill Monroe. Songs include: Jealous Heart • Walking The Floor Over You • Make The World Go Away • Ruby, Don't Take Your Love To Town • Kentucky Waltz • Is It Really Over many more.
00359504 $8.95

Volume 3
Red Foley, Steve Sholes, Bob Wills, Gene Autry, Original Carter Family, Arthur Satherley, Jimmie Davis, and The Original Sons Of The Pioneers. 24 songs: Peace In The Valley • Ashes Of Love • San Antonio Rose • Tumbling Tumble Weeds • Born To Lose • Worried Man's Blues • many more.
00359508 $8.95

Volume 4
Features: Chet Atkins, Patsy Cline, Owen Bradley, Kitty Wells, Hank Snow, Hubert Long, Connie B. Gay and Lefty Frizzell. Song highlights: Crazy • I'm Sorry • Making Believe • Wings Of A Dove • Saginaw, Michigan • and 16 others.
00359509 $8.95

Volume 5
Includes: Merle Travis, Johnny Cash, Grant Turner, Vernon Dalhart, Marty Robbins, Roy Horton, "Little" Jimmie Dickens. 19 selections: Sixteen Tons • Folsom Prison Blues • El Paso • Mockingbird Hill • May The Bird of Paradise.
00359512 $7.95

THE BEST COUNTRY SONGS EVER
We've updated this outstanding collection of country songs to include even more of your favorites—over 75 in all! Featuring: Always On My Mind • Behind Closed Doors • Could I Have This Dance • Crazy • Daddy Sang Bass • D-I-V-O-R-C-E • Forever And Ever, Amen • God Bless The U.S.A. • Grandpa (Tell Me 'Bout The Good Old Days) • Help Me Make It Through The Night • I Fall To Pieces • It We Make It Through December • Jambalaya (On The Bayou) • Love Without End, Amen • Mammas Don't Let Your Babies Grow Up To Be Cowboys • Stand By Your Man • Through The Years and more. Features stay-open binding.
00359135 $15.95

THE GREAT AMERICAN COUNTRY SONGBOOK
The absolute best collection of of top country songs anywhere. 70 titles, featuring: Any Day Now • Could I Have This Dance • Heartbroke • I Was Country When Country Wasn't Cool • I'm Gonna Hire A Wino To Decorate Our Home • It's Hard To Be Humble • Jambalaya • Smokey Mountain Rain • Through The Years • many others.
00359947 $12.95

COUNTRY LOVE SONGS
25 Sentimental country favorites, including: Could I Have This Dance • Forever And Ever, Amen • She Believes In Me • Through The Years • The Vows Go Unbroken • You Decorated My Life • You Needed Me • and more.
00311528 $9.95

Hal Leonard Publishing Corporation
For more information, see your local music dealer, or write to:
P.O. Box 13819, Milwaukee, Wisconsin 53213

Prices, availability and contents subject to change without notice.
Prices may vary outside the U.S.A.

#1 COUNTRY SONGS OF THE 80'S
44 Chart-topping country hits, including: American Made • Any Day Now • Could I Have This Dance • Crying My Heart Out Over You • Forever And Ever Amen • Forty Hour Week (For A Livin') • Grandpa (Tell Me 'Bout The Good Old Days) • He Stopped Loving Her Today • I Was In The Stream • My Heroes Have Always Been Cowboys • Smoky Mountain Rain • Why Not Me • You're The Reason God Made Oklahoma.
00360715 $12.95

80'S LADIES—TOP HITS FROM COUNTRY WOMEN OF THE 80'S
23 songs by today's female country stars including: Roseanne Cash, Crystal Gayle, The Judds, Reba McEntire, Anne Murray, K.T. Oslin and others. Songs include: I Don't Know Why You Don't Want Me • Lyin' In His Arms Again • Why Not Me • A Sunday Kind Of Love • Could I Have This Dance • Do'Ya • Strong Enough To Bend.
00359741 $9.95

THE AWARD-WINNING SONGS OF THE COUNTRY MUSIC ASSOCIATION First Edition
All of the official top five songs nominated for the CMA "Song Of The Year" from 1967 to 1983. 85 selections, featuring: Always On My Mind • Behind Closed Doors • Don't It Make My Brown Eyes Blue • Elvira • The Gambler • I.O.U. • Mammas Don't Let Your Babies Grow Up To Be Cowboys • Swingin' You're The Reason God Made Oklahoma.
00359485 $16.95

AWARD-WINNING SONGS OF THE COUNTRY MUSIC ASSOCIATION Second Edition
An update to the first edition, this songbook features 18 songs nominated for "Song of the Year" by the Country Music Association from 1984 through 1987. Songs include: Islands In The Stream • To All The Girls I've Loved Before • God Bless The U.S.A. • Seven Spanish Angels • Grandpa (Tell Me 'Bout The Good Old Days) • On The Other Hand • All My Ex's Live In Texas • Forever And Ever, Amen.
00359486 $8.95

THE NEW ULTIMATE COUNTRY FAKE BOOK
More than 700 of the greatest country hits of all-time. Includes an alphabetical index and an artist index! Includes: Cold, Cold Heart • Crazy • Crying My Heart Out Over You • Daddy Sang Bass • Diggin' Up Bones • God Bless The U.S.A. • Grandpa (Tell Me 'Bout The Good Old Days) • Green, Green Grass Of Home • He Stopped Loving Her Today • I.O.U. • I Was Country When Country Wasn't Cool • I Wouldn't Have Missed It For The World • Lucille • Mammas Don't Let Your Babies Grow Up To Be Cowboys • On The Other Hand • Ruby, Don't Take Your Love To Town • Swingin' • Talking In Your Sleep • Through The Years • Whoever's In New England • Why Not Me • You Needed Me • and MORE!
00240049 $35.00

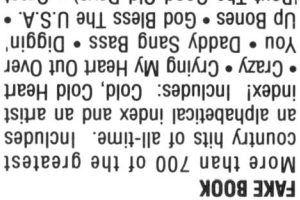